The Dog that Saved My Life

ISABEL GEORGE was born in Shropshire, where her family encouraged her early passion for animals and history. A degree in English and History opened a door to the public relations department of veterinary charity PDSA. Having the opportunity to work with the pet bravery awards and meeting veterans of battles long since fought, the idea for *The Dog that Saved My Life* was born.

Isabel now lives on the Shropshire–Staffordshire border with her three children, two hamsters and an almost-human Jack Russell, fox terrier cross called Scrumptious.

ISABEL GEORGE

The Dog that Saved My Life

Sacrifice. Loyalty. Love beyond all bounds.

HarperElement

An imprint of HarperCollins*Publishers*

77–85 Fulham Palace Road,

Hammersmith, London W6 8JB

www.harpercollins.co.uk

and *HarperElement* are trademarks of

HarperCollins*Publishers* Ltd

First published by HarperElement 2010

This production 2013

© Isabel George 2010

ISBN 978–0–00–733920–4

Printed and bound in Great Britain by
Clays Ltd, St Ives plc

MIX

Paper from
responsible sources

FSC **FSC™ C007454**
www.fsc.org

FSC™ is a non-profit international organisation established to promote
the responsible management of the world's forests. Products carrying the
FSC label are independently certified to assure consumers that they come
from forests that are managed to meet the social, economic and
ecological needs of present and future generations,
and other controlled sources.

Find out more about HarperCollins and the environment at
www.harpercollins.co.uk/green

Contents

To my children Luke, Lydia and Jamie … for their encouragement and for never tiring of these wonderful stories.

Introduction

It's one of life's little secrets, the bravery of animals in conflict.

Animals have accompanied man into battle since war was first waged. Over two thousand years ago Hannibal took war elephants, soldiers and supplies over the Alps. The giant animals negotiated narrow snow-covered mountain passes, risking life and limb to face the mighty Roman army. Centuries before that, the Ancient Egyptians recorded in their intricate paintings how they proceeded into battle with hundreds of horses pulling chariots, men holding hungry lions straining at the leash and falconers with trained hawks poised to do harm. The animals were there to play their part in the many military confrontations fought to secure supremacy.

Since those times, many stories have been told of the bears, camels, cats, dolphins, monkeys, mules, pigeons, rats and other creatures that have served with the Armed Forces during both world wars and beyond. Some were trained to perform specific tasks, like the dolphins deployed to detect underwater explosives, the pigeons released to deliver vital messages, mules laden with valuable supplies and rats sent running in tunnels to lay communication cables on the front line. Many others were present as mascots; the bears, cats and canaries were not trained to perform any role in particular but provided heart-felt companionship, warmth and humour, and helped create an incredible morale. Many animals have fulfilled this role, but perhaps none more universally and consistently than the dog.

The five stories featured in this book represent the devotion and unquestioning loyalty of the canine companion in the darkest days of war. From the life-saving actions of a Second World War Army mascot under fire to the undoubted trust shared between the Tracker dog and his handler during the war in Vietnam. Man's best friend is a constant in an uncertain environment and a welcome friend. They are a testament to companionship and to partnership when lives depend on them.

Dogs continue to prove themselves to be fearlessly loyal in all theatres of war, from the hidden depths of jungle warfare in Vietnam and Malaya to the guard and patrol duties of a desert dog in Iraq or Afghanistan. Unlike the horses of the First World War dragged down in the mud of Flanders' fields, the dog's speed and agility has always made him an asset on any battlefield. Intelligent and obedient, the dog could be the perfect messenger, able to skip over the trenches or through a minefield faster than any man. Not only are they more successful at such tasks than a human but they, although it hurts to say it, are also far more dispensable. That has always been and will continue to be a fact of wartime life. If a dog detects a landmine he is unlikely to be harmed and his actions will protect all around him. A man is unlikely to be so lucky.

Whether dropped by parachute into enemy country, helicoptered in and out of war zones, or transported in armoured vehicles, dogs have shown their versatility in war. Dogs do what's required of them and their keen sense of loyalty keeps them faithful to their duties and their military masters. Considering that the majority of the dogs recruited for service in both world wars were pet dogs donated for war service, their sacrifice was immeasurable. They were loaned to the War Office, trained for duty and distributed to the Armed Forces after 12 weeks' training. The dogs then served their country, and if they survived they were returned to their owner. These dogs took this all in their stride and the lucky ones returned to life as a fireside pet in peacetime. But for every treasured family pet to be returned home safely, there were countless others who died alongside their comrades. And for all these canine heroes, there were young soldiers, sailors and airmen who had faced horror and death and who had seen those around them lost forever, who had taken immense comfort and support from these brave, devoted companions.

The war dog is not just a feature of conflicts past. Dogs are still used in contemporary warfare and have seen service in Bosnia, Kosovo, Iraq and Afghanistan. Guard and patrol dogs remain an essential element of life on any military base at home and overseas but the role of the Arms and Explosives Search dog is one that has recently come to the fore. Trained to detect and locate weapons, explosives and bomb-making equipment, these dogs are life-savers on a daily basis. They protect the life of their handler and save the lives of military and civilian personnel with each successful 'find'. Dogs may still be listed as 'equipment' but no machine and no man can match the skill of a trained search dog. Wartime strategies and hardware may come and go but the skill of a war dog remains constant and irreplaceable.

Within the ranks, the war dog is regarded as nothing less than a fellow 'soldier', a colleague and a companion. Over the years Service dogs and mascot dogs have been decorated for their life-saving bravery in conflict.

Many have lost their lives in saving others and their fellow soldiers have deemed it vital to recognize their incredible service and sacrifice to mankind.

For these animals to give so much when they are innocent in the ways of the world and war deserves recognition. These are just five stories of many, and all are awe inspiring and heart warming in equal measure. Maybe even the dogs would ask for them to be told, and they deserve to be remembered – for all time.

Gander –

Our Best Pal

'No two-legged soldier did his duty any
better and none died more heroically than
Sergeant Gander.'

(George MacDonnell, Hong Kong Veterans Association of Canada)

'You know Pal, you're quite a handful these days. If you get much bigger we are going to have to move house!' Rod Hayden laughed as he hugged the huge, black Newfoundland dog and looked into his dewy brown eyes.

Pal drooled with pleasure as he slumped down onto his master's feet. He couldn't help being such a big dog; after all, Newfoundlands are built that way, their thick, shaggy, black coats being the perfect protection against the freezing chills of the cruel Canadian winters. Clearly Rod Hayden loved Pal and so did his son, Jack. The dog and the boy were so close that it was sometimes like having two boisterous children around the house with only one of them having a huge fur coat. Pal was adored by his family and by every child in the town of Gander, Newfoundland.

When the snow fell on Gander it fell hard and heavy. A good snowfall would block the doorway to the house and cover the roads so perfectly that they simply ceased to exist. In the worst of it, snow banks would rise higher than the roof-tops and venturing outdoors meant piling on as much clothing as it was possible to wear under an insulated top coat. But, for the children, the most exciting thing about the snow was sledding. And who was always around to join in the fun? Pal.

Pal, who was only two years old and already almost the size of a small pony, had given Rod Hayden an idea. A while back he had seen a set of pony reins hanging on a hook in the attic and now seemed a good time to put them to good use. He had no idea where they had come from nor how old they were. He had lived in the house over ten years and had never owned a pony or a trap. The rocky tracks that meandered off the main roads in Newfoundland were unsuitable for the small hooves of a pony or the delicate wheels of a cart. But wherever they had come from and however long they had been in that dusty box in the attic didn't matter now. Rod knew exactly what he had to do and he knew that Jack and his friends would be so excited.

It didn't take long to persuade Pal to try on the customized harness Rod had adapted from the pony bridle. The padded band designed to go over the pony's broad muzzle was a perfect fit and the long, covered straps slipped comfortably around the dog's body. The reins were short to suit a child's small hands and Jack couldn't wait to try them out.

Ten-year-old Jack watched his father attach Pal's new harness to the sled and he could see the dog was just as keen as he was to get out into the snow. Pal had never worn anything like reins before. He had never even worn a dog lead, but this big, friendly giant was happy to do whatever Rod Hayden wanted him to and so, after what probably seemed like forever to the young Jack, the sled and Pal were ready. 'Come on Pal, let's go!' said Jack, raising the reins as Pal lurched forward with the sled lumbering behind him.

By the time he reached his friend Eileen's house, Jack was handling the reins with confidence and he was looking forward to showing her his clever dog in harness.

But in the small community of Gander it didn't take long for every child in walking distance of the Haydens' house to hear that Pal was giving sled rides. Soon Eileen was just one of several children queuing up to take her turn to 'drive'. Waving and shrieking with laughter, Jack and his friends dashed along and Pal pranced around like a show pony, his long pink tongue lolling out of his mouth. No one had ever seen anything like it before.

When he wasn't playing in the snow or taking up space in the house, Pal found a new pastime as Gander became a focus for wartime activity.

Newfoundland Airport, as it was known, had been constructed in 1936 and two years later it boasted four paved, fully operational runways. Not only was it one of the world's largest airbases at the time but by 1940 its geographical location made it one of the most strategically important. It was North America's most eastern-based airport and therefore perfectly placed to be a refuelling depot for transatlantic flights, and it would also give pilots the greatest range for surveillance flights over the Western Atlantic. All the Allies had to do was secure it and protect it from a possible German attack.

In 1941, the Dominion of Newfoundland offered the Royal Canadian Air Force (RCAF) operational control of the airport. Suddenly the town of Gander was no longer just a random collection of 10 houses, a one-roomed school and an airstrip surrounded by several shed-like buildings. The Second World War was about to transform this isolated town into a strategic military airbase and place at its hub the operational activities of the RCAF. Ferry Command, the organization responsible for transporting new aircraft across the Atlantic to supply the Allied forces fighting the war in Europe, constructed a base there. The Royal Canadian Navy also selected Gander as an ideal base for a radio transmission centre and a 'listening post' to pick up German U-boat radio transmissions to and from Germany. Any information that could help pinpoint the position of enemy U-boats was crucial at the time as the U-boats were proving to be devastatingly successful in the war at sea.

Initially a detachment from Canada's Black Watch regiment was posted to Gander to defend the base from enemy attack. Later the Americans also sent troops. Gander had become too important a base to risk losing or incurring any damage from enemy activity. From then on, operating as Gander Airfield, the base came to life with more hangers, more equipment, more personnel, longer runways and additions like a laundry, a bakery and a hospital.

Rod Hayden, his wife and young son Jack were one of very few families living in Gander. Jack attended the local school with 13 other children, while his father, depot manager for the Shell Oil Company, was responsible for refuelling the aircraft bound for England. This had become a 24-hour programme of activity and it would have been a lonely job if it hadn't been for Pal, Rod's canine shadow.

The Hayden family home was adjacent to the runway and for an excitable dog with energy to release, this was just another playground. Running to meet the planes as they landed was something Pal loved to do before he dashed to the cockpit to sit with the crew. The dog wasn't always a welcome visitor. But that didn't bother Pal. There were so many planes and crews going in and out of Gander that he had plenty of chances to play his tricks on unsuspecting pilots.

Often, as the ground staff worked frantically to clear the runway of snow, Pal would wait patiently for the lights to appear, illuminating the landing strip. For him it was the sign that an aircraft was on its way in and he prepared himself to greet the crew. Severe weather conditions were always a challenge to a pilot's concentration and a row of coloured lights stretching forward to welcome the aircraft out of a snow-filled sky was a reassuring sight. No one could afford to take chances. Lives were at risk. Pal's unscheduled 'welcomes' could be too much of a surprise for many pilots, and quite often the control tower person-nel would receive a message that there was a 'bear on the runway'! The operators knew what they meant and replied, 'No. That's not a bear. That's Pal. He's a dog!'

Pal was a good name for this huge, friendly dog. He was everyone's friend and in the spring of 1941 his list of friends grew overnight when a battalion of the Royal Rifles of Canada was posted to Gander Airfield for airfield protection and security duty.

As they lived on the airbase itself the soldiers became Pal's neighbours and they happily shared their food – and even their beer – with him. They taught him tricks like how to stand on his back legs and put his paws on their shoulders. They encouraged him to take showers; which, being a Newfoundland dog, he loved. However no one ever tried to wake Pal when he decided to take a nap in one of the bunks. He hated being woken up and it was the only time he displayed irritation or anything like a bad temper. The men learned very quickly to 'leave this sleeping dog to lie' as long as he liked.

Pal was a happy dog. He liked people and people liked him. But his size sometimes made him clumsy and one day while he was out with the children on the sled, Pal jumped up to greet Eileen Chafe's sister Joan and accidently scratched her face deeply. Pal knew immediately that he had done something wrong and he licked her hand to tell her he was sorry. Although the little girl wasn't seriously hurt, Rod Hayden took it as a sign that Pal had outgrown his time as a children's playmate and that, combined with his often dangerous antics at the airfield, made him decide to give Pal away at the first opportunity.

So it was that Pal moved from being a family pet to becoming a military mascot. He would even have his own bunk in the barracks with the Royal Rifles. Even Jack Hayden understood that the mascot idea was a perfect solution and, the next day, Pal moved in with his new friends. He settled into his new life very quickly but he still enjoyed daily visits from the local children, and especially Jack, who missed his dog very much.

Outside of the world of Gander Airfield the war was well advanced and the soldiers sensed they might be posted overseas any day. But there was something they had to do before they left. Their mascot dog was so much a part of the place where they were stationed that the men decided to give Pal a new name that would always be a reminder of home. They decided to call their soldier dog – Gander.

Just days later the men received the news they had been expecting. They were to leave immediately: Destination – unknown.

By October 1941 the Second World War was moving into its third year and Adolf Hitler's Germany was achieving far-flung military success and extending its power. The Führer's indomitable general, Erwin Rommel, had the desert campaign in North Africa well under the

German Army's control. At sea, German U-boats continued to threaten British merchant shipping bringing vital
supplies across the Atlantic and on land the German
Army, motivated and encouraged by repeated military
success, was marching across Europe, effortlessly over-
coming all opposition. In that month almost all of Western Europe and much of Soviet Russia was under the
military heel of Germany and its Nazi leaders.

Germany's ever-tightening grip on Europe cast an
ominous shadow over a free Britain. Only his obsession
with completing the invasion of Russia could divert
Hitler's attention away from the final unconquered
parts of the Continent as he prepared to march his
army to the very gates of Moscow. He appeared to be
ruling supreme, his armies were unstoppable and
unconquerable, and the rest of the world seemed to
have been reduced to a crowd of powerless and quiv-
ering spectators.

Japan, however, had its own ambitions. As Hitler's
divisions powered their way across Europe, Emperor
Hirohito was not so secretly strengthening Japanese
forces on land, at sea and in the air. The Japanese High

Command had designs on British and Dutch territorial and mineral possessions in South East Asia, and bloody battle was clearly imminent. China was already into its fourth year of occupation and continuing battle with the Emperor's invasion forces. If the British were not quick enough to substantially and meaningfully reinforce their Hong Kong territory with defensive forces, Japan would add Hong Kong to its list of conquests too.

Hong Kong was a thriving British colony, representing not only an economic jewel in the crown of British trading interests but also the pinnacle of British military power in the Far East. The Japanese War Cabinet had long been aware of Hong Kong's strategic importance to their war of conquest. The Commonwealth troops already based there represented little more than a token security presence. These soldiers might have been enough to reassure the diplomatic staff and the loyal residents living and working in Hong Kong but it was nowhere near what was required to hold off the might of a battle-hardened and proven invasion force. Despite dire warnings from some of his military and political advisers, British Prime Minister Winston Churchill focused on the battles and reverses in the Mediterranean theatre and in the air and sea at home. He had been reluctant, until that point, to send a significant force to Hong Kong. But things were changing rapidly.

Within days of receiving the order to leave their barracks near Gander Airfield, the Royal Rifles were packed and ready to move out. They had been issued with their tropical kit but had not been given a briefing on what lay ahead. There was even speculation that they might be going to North Africa. For now there was one certainty: they were taking Gander with them. It was a tall order to hide a Newfoundland dog that was almost as tall as a Shetland pony and weighed as much as a fully grown man. 'I think you've gone crazy,' said one of the civilians on the camp. 'How on earth are you going to hide that dog? You know what will happen if he's caught, don't you? They'll throw him overboard if you're at sea and if you're on the train he'll be put out at the next station. Then what'll happen to him? I think you're crazy and I think the dog needs to stay here in Gander.'

It was a brave speech but the well-meaning man was wasting his breath. He was challenging the Royal Rifles of Canada and he should have known better. Besides, who relished the idea of telling Fred Kelly, Gander's partner, that the dog wasn't going with them? That night the men called a meeting in the barracks. It was agreed that Fred would kick off with a request for a show of hands. They needed to know that they would have the support and co-operation of all the men if Gander was to leave with them. It took under five minutes for Fred to finish his speech and gain a unanimous vote of support. The dog was going with them. From that meeting a sub-committee of six people was formed. These were the people who would be Gander's closest companions and the ones directly responsible for his health and welfare. If there were any major decisions to be made, these men would make them. If there was any blame to take, these men would take it. The Royal Rifles of Canada were well aware that pets and mascots were not allowed to be taken on military duty into operational areas. This was an accepted fact in the military. If they were caught there would be severe consequences. This too was accepted.

The priority was to prepare Gander for the journey. If the posting was, as they guessed, to the Far East, it would mean hiding their huge mascot dog during a train journey that would take them several thousand miles across Canada, and on a troopship that would spend many weeks at sea. There was also the problem of rations on the journey. There was only one thing to do that would protect the dog in any semi-official way: using official and unofficial influences in the military system, Gander would have to be listed as a soldier. One of the men. A sergeant. Gander of the Royal Rifles. Not only would he be on the ration strength he would also have a rank that would appear on all the transport-movement papers.

'Sergeant' Gander was issued with his own kitbag too. It contained all he needed for a comfortable journey and protection in battle: a special dog brush, a towel, soap, water and food bowls, a towel and everything a dog might need were gathered together. Gander was assigned a seat on the train and all the men had to do was make sure their dog was neither seen nor heard by the officers. If he was discovered it was almost inevitable that the men would be ordered to leave him behind or if they were at sea he could be thrown overboard. No one was going to let their friend down.

In charge of the rather hairy recruit was Rifleman Fred Kelly. Kelly had been a dog lover all his life and from the moment Fred set his eyes on Gander it was clear to everyone that it was a perfect partnership. A soldier at the age of just 19 Fred knew more about dogs than he did about fighting but he was proud of his country and ready to do what was expected of him. The men had very little training so for Fred and his fellow Royal Rifles there was a huge fear of the unknown. For all the men, Gander became a welcome distraction from the uncertainty that plagued them day and night. At least Fred had Gander to fill his thoughts and the dog's care to structure parts of his day. Gander needed his food and needed to be groomed, otherwise his huge fur coat would get matted and the discomfort might cause problems. An unhappy dog was not going to make for a silent travelling partner.

In some respects the partnership of Fred Kelly and Gander was something of a physical mismatch. Fred was not a tall man, but Gander was a very large dog so when they stood or sat together it was sometimes difficult to see where the great woolly dog ended and the small-framed man in uniform began. For the journey that lay ahead of them, this was to prove a useful element of camouflage. The men knew that if Gander was found they would never see him again.

Quebec, the home of the Royal Rifles of Canada, was proud of its sons in uniform. Mobilized in July 1940, the regiment drew most of its recruits from Eastern Quebec and Western New Brunswick, which made it an English-speaking unit, with a quarter of the recruits being bi-lingual French. Quebec City welcomed the men 'home' and arranged a parade in their honour. It was an occasion to salute the 962 men and one dog who were about to fight for their country overseas. Each man marched straight and tall behind the distinctive figures of Gander and Corporal Kelly, who led the parade. The band played and people waved their handkerchiefs and their hats to cheer the men and their faithful mascot on their way. Smoke billowed from the train awaiting the soldiers' arrival at Valcartier station as it made ready to take the troops closer to their war. But it was only right that after the marching, Gander should take a shower. Somehow Fred managed to locate one and the hot dog was able to enjoy his last shower for a good while.

Smoke from the train swirled around as the guards and officers mingled with civilians and soldiers on the busy platform. Fred Kelly and his friends viewed the situation and tried not to look as nervous as they felt. The officers were on the look out for deserters or anyone trying to smuggle an animal mascot aboard. If only Gander had been a monkey or a kitten or something smaller than a full-grown Newfoundland dog, hiding him would have been easier. But the men were just about to discover that their dog was the most obedient creature on earth, and the cunning plan they had hatched in the relative security of Gander Airfield was about to be put to the test.

Within seconds of marching into the station the men were lining up to board the train. Fred Kelly tightened his grip on Gander's leash as the rest of the detachment mingled to shield the dog from view. Gander wasn't used to crowds like this and Fred could sense the big dog's unease. All the time they were hoping no one would look down and see four hairy black paws on the ground.

Roll call sent shivers down Fred Kelly's spine. But he need not have worried. It was to go just as they had practised. Whenever Sergeant Gander's name was called, Fred piped up 'Sir!' and two of his friends started a scuffle to distract the officers while the dog was bundled onto the train. The plan worked perfectly! Now all they had to do was find their seats before any official took a backwards glance to double-check the large fur-coated recruit with the lumbering walk.

Although Sergeant Gander had a seat on the train, Fred decided to err on the side of caution and kept Gander lying on the floor for the time being. The dog was used to the floor; if he couldn't get a bunk he would lie quietly at his master's feet. The noise and bustle of the officers and men of the Royal Rifles of Canada and the 911 Winnipeg Grenadiers who boarded the train were enough to disguise the sound of the mascot dog's heavy panting. But from this point on, the men had one thought – making sure their mascot stayed with them all the way. Fred Kelly's caring approach and the tone of his voice saying, 'That's it, Gander old chum ... quiet now ... good boy ...' reassured the big dog that he was in safe hands.

The train was scheduled to stop in Ottawa, its third stop on the journey to Vancouver on the west coast. Brigadier Lawson, a veteran of the First World War, stationed in Canada's capital and a career soldier, was to board the train as commander of 'C' Force – the newly created fighting force comprising the Winnipeg Grenadiers, the Royal Rifles of Canada, attached military support personnel and one mascot dog called Gander.

It was a three-day train journey and Gander was the perfect travelling companion. There was not an awful lot for a dog to do on a train and the men were afraid Gander would get bored and noisy and blow his cover but, as always, the fears can be greater than the reality. While the men played cards or disappeared into their own worlds to write letters to loved ones, Gander stayed with them. Sometimes he chose a lap to lie on or, if someone left their seat for too long, he would stretch out and fall asleep for a while or at least until the rightful owner gave Gander a gentle nudge to leave. No one minded Gander plonking his big slobbering jaws on their lap. If he decided you were going to be the play partner for the day it was best to give into it because he would never let a soldier have any peace until they had played at least one game of tug of war with a sock. The most difficult part about having Gander along for the ride was the impossibility of taking him for walks. Gander was very patient but he was a big dog and it wasn't good to keep him cooped up in the train, but the men had no choice. They had come this far, so they made sure that Gander had long play sessions with improvised toys and a huge amount of tickles and play fights. Unable to enjoy his favourite thing of all, a shower, Fred ensured that he was washed down and that he had long grooming sessions too. Toileting was difficult for Gander because at almost three years old he was used to looking after himself. This was like puppy training all over again. The good thing was, Fred Kelly was used to dogs and had the inbuilt patience to coach Gander through the necessary paces. He also had to have everyone else's support to make it work and in case of 'accidents'. Fred created a toilet area for Gander in one of the washrooms. After a few days it was clear what he needed to perform and when, so Fred accompanied the dog and dealt with it all. It was rare that anyone else had anything to do as Gander was very 'regular' and Fred was never far away. If there was the odd accident the men knew what to do.

But another challenge lay ahead. Arriving in Vancouver on 28 October the men found the troopships, the HMNZS *Awatea* and HMCS *Prince Robert*, docked and waiting for them to embark. Before the war the massive and majestic *Awatea*, a converted luxury liner, had run between her home in New Zealand and Canada. Now her state rooms accommodated the officers while the men, the majority of them Winnipeg Grenadiers, slung their hammocks in every available space, even above the mess tables. The remainder of 'C' Force, the Royal Rifles of Canada, boarded the HMCS *Prince Robert*, the escort vessel, and Gander was amongst them.

The dockhands were busy loading the crates of supplies and ammunition, and the area was heaving with the hustle and bustle of dockyard activity. It was just the kind of chaos the men needed. Who was going to notice one dog in a muddled crowd like that? They just needed to get Sergeant Gander through one more roll call and they would soon be on the open sea.

As the men boarded the HMCS *Prince Robert*, they gathered to hide Gander as best they could. Just as before, they walked very closely together, Gander between them, and marched up to the gangplank. The stevedores noticed the dog, however, and refused to allow 'the bear' onto the boat. The regimental officers agreed but the men howled in protest when it was discovered that one of the officers had been allowed to take his small pet dog. The men pointed out that Gander was simply a large dog, so the authorities relented and Gander boarded the ship. They were home and dry! Gander was as exhausted as the men, who still had to hang their hammocks before they could rest. Gander couldn't wait for such a luxury. After nudging his head against some of his friends, by way of maybe saying 'thank you', he slumped down onto the cabin floor and fell fast asleep. No one was going to move that huge slumbering dog, even though he was right in the middle of the accommodation area. So, they covered him with a blanket and left him in peace.

Several hours later Gander bolted out of his sleep to find that he was surrounded by his soldier friends. It was another new environment and he seemed some-what unsteady on his feet as the ship rolled and swayed a little in the water. Fred was quick to move to give the dog a hug and say, 'It's all right Gander. You're on a troopship and, like the rest of us buddy, you're on your way to war.' The men had guessed before the official announcement was made that they were bound for the Far East. Departing from Vancouver had been the biggest clue and now they were about four weeks from entering a war zone.

The entire regiment and now the crew of the *Prince Robert* knew the dog was onboard, so it was decided to allow Gander to enjoy the freedom of the ship at last. But how best to do that? Fred suggested that Gander make his entrance the next morning away from land; the thought of another long, uneventful day ahead would be brightened when the soldiers saw Gander. And so as the men finished their breakfast next morning Fred chose his moment to release Gander, when the men were chatting and finishing the dregs of their coffee. The big dog trotted into the mess area and immediately picked on a few of the men to brush up to and plant his great web-footed paws on! It was a great moment for all the men to see their mascot looking so fit and healthy and full of fun. He was the morale boost they needed at this stage of their journey. He 'rough and tumbled' with them and slobbered on them, commandeered their hammocks for a sleep and begged anything they cared to give him from their meagre rations. Gander was on the way to war amongst the men he loved and they, in return, loved him for it!

It was hot and uncomfortable in the cramped quarters of the HMCS *Prince Robert*. Gander probably felt it most of all and there was little that Fred Kelly could do to cool the big dog down, especially as there was a shortage of water on board and they needed every drop for drinking. The dog was now the most popular soldier aboard and his fellow soldiers did what they could to help him settle. But when his panting got bad all he could do was find a breezy companionway to lie in. The men knew if they saw Gander lying down it was a cool spot and they would often join him.

It was going to take four weeks for the troopships to reach the island of Hong Kong. It was a long journey but Gander was good company and a happy distraction for the men. Many were very young, some just 16 years old and away from home for the first time. All of them were proud to be fighting for their country and for freedom, but at the same time terrified of what lay ahead. For now they were on a voyage where the hours were filled with playing card games and any kind of activity to distract everyone from the smothering heat and the rolling of the ship. Conditions were the same on both troopships but it was fortunate that Gander was on the smaller vessel as there were fewer bodies around and it was possible to find a space away from every other hot person on board. Now that he was able to walk the ship freely, it was a great relief to the men who had sheltered him for so long and a bigger relief for Gander. It meant that Gander could perform another duty on the ship, that of ship's comforter. Being in the presence of such a young crew, Gander was with men who were afraid they might never see home again. Many of them had never travelled outside their home towns in Canada; now they were heading for part of a country that they knew nothing about, and which did not share their culture or their way of thinking. They might fight an enemy on this foreign battlefield and perhaps that is where they would fight and die. So it was that Gander became a great comfort to the men of the Royal Rifles just by being around them. He reminded many soldiers of their dogs back home and provided that vital psychological link to the memory of home comforts, of a dog stretched out on the family hearth.

At sea, with no sighting of another ship for days, news of the world beyond the troopships gave the soldiers a glimpse of what was going to face them in Hong Kong. Tensions ran high in the confines of the ship as news of world conflict and worrying developments at their destination reached them. Soon they had their first glimpse of land since hitting the open sea. The view was dim and hazy but behind the cloudbank lay the craggy coastline of the Philippines. During the journey one of the men had become ill and died in the early hours. In the mists of morning the men gathered on the deck for a service that ended with a burial at sea. Later that same day, they reached Manila harbour. American fighter planes patrolled the skies, protecting US warships docked in readiness for an order to defend US interests in the event of an outbreak of hostilities and to engage any Japanese invaders. It was a sobering sight seeing so much hardware ready and waiting to be used in the event of war. The troopships *Awatea* and *Prince Robert* looked small and insignificant alongside the grey giants of the US Navy. Rising up out of the water like menacing sea monsters, they boosted the confidence of the Canadian soldiers looking on. Just seeing them ready and waiting was a strange comfort to the young men. Taking on oil and water, the troopships sailed out, giving the men one last view of the mountain peaks shrouded in cloud. Forty-eight hours later the men had been issued with their rifles and steel helmets and were preparing to disembark at what was to be their last port of call for a long time.

As dawn broke on 16 November 1941, the *Awatea* and the *Prince Rupert* rolled in the swell of the South

China Sea as the men of 'C' Force, accompanied by two nursing sisters and several personnel from Brigade Headquarters, caught sight of the Hong Kong shore-line. As they stood on deck watching the activity ashore, everyone remembered and understood why, for several days, they had been drilling, exercising and familiarizing themselves with the equipment. There had been no time for card games of late. The Bren guns had been unpacked and training had begun. Dismantling, assembling, loading, firing, cleaning and caring for their guns and rifles were drilled into the young soldiers. Drilled in because their lives, very definitely, were going to depend on it.

Just the sight of dry land was a relief to everyone aboard, and Fred thought Gander must have felt it too. Sitting at Fred's feet he looked excited and kept looking back to Fred, perhaps asking, 'Are we there now? Is this where I can smell the grass again and have a shower and a beer?' Even with the sting of saltwater still on his face and its taste on his tongue, he seemed happy to see other ships and other signs of life beyond the confines of the *Prince Rupert*. Feeling the dog straining at the leash,

Fred would probably have said, 'Calm down now Gander, it won't be long until you can get off this ship and sleep in a proper bed. You must not get too excited now. We still have things to do to keep you safe.'

As Fred accompanied Gander down the gangplank and onto the dockside he could feel the leash pull even harder. Gander had sensed freedom and it felt to Fred as if he was going to make a dash for it. If there was one thing Fred couldn't afford to happen now, it was for Gander to break loose on the dockside. The mayhem it would cause would draw unnecessary attention to the dog and, after all they had been through, they were not going to let that happen. Also, if Gander dashed off now he would not have a clue where he was and there would be no time to locate him. Fred gripped the dog's leash lower and stronger. He had already read the dog's mind. He could tell that, to Gander, the expanse of water between the ship and the dockside must have looked like a giant bath. And Gander, who had really missed his showers and baths over the past months, just might take a dive. 'Hey, don't go thinking that water is a bath for you Gander,' said Fred, who grabbed the dog tightly and pulled him back from the edge of the dock. He couldn't help chuckling at the cheekiness of the big dog, who often acted like a mischievous child! 'Buddy, if you could read the signs in the harbour telling of the cholera in there you would think twice about jumping in the water! Don't worry, we'll soon have you washed down and spruced up when we get to the barracks.'

The entire population of Kowloon turned out to greet the soldiers. And as he watched the sea of Union Jacks fluttering and heard the crowd cheering, Gander lifted his head and trotted proudly, in Fred's capable hands, to take his place at the head of the Royal Rifles. It was a real carnival atmosphere as the residents of Hong Kong turned out to welcome the soldiers to the city. A pipe band from the Royal Scots Guards garrison was there to meet the troopships and lead the parade with Gander and the rest of 'C' Force proudly marching on dry land for the first time in four weeks. It was a proud moment for the men and their mascot dog. Gander was receiving lots of attention, especially from the children in the crowd. Fred heard later that a lot of the women and children through Gander was a bear so they held back at first, not knowing if he might eat them rather than lick them. Once they realized the big, hairy mascot was a mild-mannered dog they flocked to stroke and make friends with him. It had been some time since Gander had enjoyed the playful attention of children and he hadn't forgotten how to be gentle with them or how to have fun.

The parade would take the men to Sham Shui Po Barracks, which were to be the new home and training ground for 'C' Force. The dazzling white of the barrack buildings and the lushness of the oriental gardens were a welcome sight to the men who, for several weeks, had only seen the gloomy interior of the troopship. It didn't take long for Gander to sniff out the showers and remind Fred of his promise of a cooling wash. It was a promise Fred was happy to keep for his friend, who had already taken to lying on the cold shower-room floor to escape the sticky heat. Through the weeks of travelling the men had dreamed of swapping their hammocks for beds and here the relative comfort of a barrack cot caused great excitement. True to form, the men held back while Gander chose the bed he wanted and then everyone else made their choice from what was left. It was a good way to start but everyone knew that Gander would, in the end, make every bed his own and he was just too big to argue with!

Life within Sham Shui Po Barracks was more than comfortable and the local Chinese population were happy to shine shoes, make beds and run errands for a chance to earn a few Canadian dollars. (A boy who earned two dollars a week would be considered a 'millionaire'.) The arrival of the Canadians was good for the local economy and for morale. No one really believed the Japanese would have the audacity to invade this Crown Colony but they felt safer, all the same, to have the increased military presence. What the locals probably didn't realize was that in terms of numbers and equipment the island was still poorly defended. On paper there were now over 14,500 military personnel on the ground but this figure included several senior nursing staff, St John Ambulance representatives and the Hong Kong Mule Corps. When Kowloon welcomed the Royal Rifles and the Winnipeg Grenadiers the sight of the men in uniform reinforced the notion that Hong Kong was immune to invasion.

To a large extent, the life of the native people carried on as normal. It was the cool season and the mud flats close to the garrison were a hive of industry, with locals digging for clams. In the town their daily working lives continued, and the lively nightlife of theatres and bars hummed with the sound of laughter.

There was time for the men and Gander to familiarize themselves with the area and the equipment being delivered for the defence of the island. The Bren guns that would be used on the border with Japanese-occupied China were made ready, along with the rifles, shells and grenades. Constructing the dugouts, shelters and pillboxes that were to be the primary line of defence was a priority and, even in the stifling heat, three sessions of guard duty and two hours of morning parade became part of the daily routine. Gander accompanied the men on patrol and whenever Fred Kelly was on guard duty Gander was sure to follow. The big black dog enjoyed being on duty, as long as he could take a nap in the shade when the mood took him.

And at night Gander would join the men in the pill-boxes. They felt safer having Gander beside them.

Given the beautiful surroundings the men could not be blamed for sometimes thinking they might be spared the hostility of conflict. Gander adapted well to the life of a soldier dog on a pass. It was not unusual for him to accept a bottle of beer from one of his many friends and an invitation to shower in their washroom several times a day. He lounged on their cots, shared their rations, enjoyed being groomed and played with and generally treated as a VIP. Fred was never far from Gander's side if he could help it. When the men were on parade or on a training session and Gander was not allowed to join them, it was Fred who made the dog comfortable while they were away. For Fred it was a little like having a child to care for, only this 'child' liked to hog the shower and drink beer out of a sink. He also liked to help out where he could and if there was a job that needed a dog to pull an ammunition cart, Gander got the job. Looking after Gander could have been a full-time job but Fred had it down to a fine art a little while after they were partnered in Canada. He could almost think ahead of the big dog and that came in useful, particularly after showers. Fred learnt that if you didn't get out of the way fast enough Gander would shake and cover you in water, but you also had to be double-quick and catch him and dry him off before he headed out to roll in the dirt. As soon as Fred caught up with Gander the dog would stop Fred in his tracks by standing on his hind legs and planting his paws firmly on Fred's shoulders.

His relationship with the local Chinese population was not so friendly. It started after the parade on the day Gander and his friends arrived. Fred and several Royal Rifles were walking with Gander near to the barracks when they were approached by two men who were paying particular interest to Gander. They seemed friendly and Fred thought he had no reason to be suspicious. But then one of the men started to run and Gander decided to follow him. The other man then ran after Gander. By the time Fred and his friends arrived on the scene it was obvious the men had tried to pull and push Gander through a hole in a fence and had only succeeded in scaring the dog. Immediately, Fred dashed in to take Gander back to the camp while the others made it clear to the two gentlemen that Gander was off limits. They never had trouble again. But the encounter was enough for Gander to decide on a dislike for the look and sound of the local people. He must have thought they would all try to drag him away. The word on the street was that the dog was destined for the dinner table, so it was good that his friends were soon on the scene to rescue him. From that day on, Gander treated all Chinese people with suspicion. He was automatically wary and if they approached him he would growl and bare his teeth.

For a while life in the barracks was calm and slightly unreal but by mid November (19 November according to a veteran's account) news reached the Hong Kong garrison that the Japanese Army was only 23 miles away. In October the Japanese had moved over 20,000 troops in Southern China and a rumour that the Imperial Army was about to move several thousand more troops was sounding more like fact than mere scaremongering.

On Sunday 7 December 1941, the Japanese finally showed the world their military might with a surprise attack on Pearl Harbor, the Hawaiian port that was the headquarters of the US Pacific Fleet. In one morning 353 Japanese navy aircraft from six aircraft carriers sank or damaged many US warships, destroyed 188 aircraft on the ground and killed over 2,000 US service personnel and civilians. The attack brought the Americans into the Second World War, and the war in the East was on with a vengeance.

At first light the following day, the Japanese Army set its sights on Hong Kong. Gander's war had begun.

General Maltby, Commander of the British Garrison in Hong Kong, who was now fully convinced of the Japanese intent to invade Hong Kong, gave the order to activate the garrison. Maltby had always feared that the Japanese would launch a seaborne attack, which explained the concentration of defences on the south of the island. The north side, facing the mainland, was less well fortified; this area included the Lye Mun Gap, which at its narrowest point was only 450 yards across. In an attempt to cover as much ground as possible the general decided to split his defences. West Brigade, comprising the Winnipeg Grenadiers, was commanded by Brigadier Lawson. Gander and the rest of 'C' Force formed part of East Brigade, under Brigadier Wallis. They were to be stationed in the Lye Mun region, with three company platoons and four reinforcement platoons. Scattered amongst them were small detachments of the Scots Guards, the Middlesex Regiment, the Hong Kong Defence Corps, and the Rajputs and Punjabis of the Indian Army.

After news broke of the attack on Pearl Harbor the men had been confined to barracks. As a result of a breakdown in communications, Gander and the men had no idea that the battle for Hong Kong had begun just hours after the Japanese attack. The first the British heard of it was when an Intelligence Officer assigned to monitoring the Japanese broadcasts picked up the following message at 4.45 a.m on 8 December 1941:

The Army and Navy division of Imperial Headquarters jointly announced at six o'clock this morning (Tokyo time), December 8, that the Imperial Army and Navy forces have begun hostilities against the American and British Forces in the Pacific at dawn today.

Within hours of receiving Maltby's orders to leave the mainland, every kitbag was packed and ammunition was being loaded onto the ferry that would take them from Kowloon to Hong Kong Island. It was the first clue the men received to there being a declaration of war. The second clue was the appearance of Japanese bombers overhead and the howl of the air-raid siren over Kowloon. Then the bombing began.

The wind and rain lashed down as the soldiers landed on the island, laden with kitbags, ammunition, supplies and a very wet Newfoundland dog. 'Come on buddy, not far to go now and we'll be home and dry,' said Fred Kelly, as he gently persuaded Gander to keep up with the rest of the Royal Rifles who were hurrying to take up their positions across 15 miles of the eastern part of the island.

Safely ashore, Gander stayed close to Fred. His dense coat hung heavy with rainwater and it slowed his pace as he clambered to keep up with his fellow soldiers. Fred was concerned that the dog might catch a chill and so he promised Gander a drying down when they reached their camp. Makeshift camps were being set up, and men and ammunition moved into position. There were not enough tents for every man there but the men were tired enough to sleep anywhere as the rumble of artillery continued throughout the night.

The assortment of coastal guns, manned pillboxes, minefields and barbed-wire fences that encircled the island came immediately under attack. The Royal Navy presence consisted of one destroyer, and the Royal Air Force retained a maximum of three torpedo bombers at Kai Tek Airport. On the morning of 8 December Japanese fighter aircraft destroyed the airport in one single attack. On their second run, the Japanese planes dropped leaflets demanding the surrender of Hong Kong. The British refused.

As the sirens wailed relentlessly and the sky filled with the darting shadows of fighter planes, the soldiers hurried to stock the wooden pillboxes that were strategically placed in a line of defence that was to protect against any landing from the sea. It was a race against time to get men and guns into place before the invaders made it ashore. It was a difficult time for Gander, who wanted to be at Fred Kelly's side every second but had to content himself with spending his time confined to the makeshift barracks. But like any other good soldier, he took his turn on watch at night.

Shells exploded all around and the sky flashed burnt orange. Huge sheets of flame carved into the inky sky as the men worked frantically to move the boxes of ammunition that still lay where the ferry had landed. With nowhere to store these vital supplies out of the driving rain, cover had to be found urgently. The pillboxes were already packed with crates of equipment but still more had to be crammed into the tiny space available. Fred decided that a pillbox was the best place for Gander while all the work was going on. Although he wasn't upset by the steady shelling that became a constant background noise, Gander liked to be so close to Fred that he was in danger of getting in the way. He didn't whine or whimper or cause his friends a problem, he just liked to be close to them. The thud of the shelling continued into the night. Exhausted and desperate for rest, the men found a space to sleep not knowing if sleep was possible.

Gander was happy to have the men around him. Fred was convinced that the dog sensed the stress of the situation and was always very good at choosing the man who looked the most tired and anxious to get his full attention. Laying his head on the man's lap, Gander heaped his full weight on too. No one wanted to move him. Wherever the dog lay, he brought a special peace and to the 'chosen' person he brought a tranquillity that was unknown in that place at that time. The dog was the perfect partner. Man's best friend. The one individual who could bring a kind of peace where peace seemed impossible.

Over the next five days the Japanese superiority in the air gave their infantry an advantage on the ground. Marching into the New Territories without opposition, a wave of khaki started to wash over the mainland. The Punjabis attempted to stem the advance by demolishing bridges and destroying road and rail links but it did not slow the enemy taking ground. By 10 December the Japanese had swarmed into and over the populated mainland city and were ready to make an approach on the island.

By the morning of 13 December, all British, Canadian and other forces that had remained on the mainland had been evacuated to Hong Kong Island as the Japanese invasion proceeded at pace. The total defence force of over 14,500 men was now on the island. Seeing this action as a retreat, the Japanese were quick to make another demand for surrender. The British governor, Sir Mark Young, refused. Determined to smash the desperate Allied defence, the Imperial Army intensified the shelling from the mainland, taking out ammunition dumps and supply depots, and wreaking havoc on the communication lines.

Wave after wave of shelling and artillery battered the island's coastal defences. The roadside pillboxes, so easy to pinpoint from the air, were systematically shelled all along the north shore, which made the line of defence strain under the attack. The Japanese advance seemed unstoppable. The area around the Lye Mun Gap, where Gander and the rest of 'C' Force were positioned, was now coming under threat. Between 10 December and the 17th, the units sustained heavy casualties, but still the British refused to surrender to the Japanese invaders. A message was sent to them:

> The Governor and Commander-in-Chief of Hong Kong declines most absolutely to enter into negotiations for the surrender of Hong Kong, and takes this opportunity of notifying Lieutenant-General Takaishi Sakai and Vice-Admiral Masaichi Nimi that he is not prepared to receive any further communications from them on the subject.

Undeterred by British defiance, Lieutenant-General Sakai issued his own declaration in response:

> On Thursday night, December 18, Japanese Imperial Forces will land upon the Island of Hong Kong at suitable situations between North Point and Lye Mun.

By late evening on 18 December 1941, the Japanese launched their attack on Hong Kong, coming thick and fast into the Lye Mun Gap. Boatload after boatload of soldiers in khaki landed, and they came screaming up the beach towards the Canadians, opening fire as they ran. There was no time for Fred Kelly to secure Gander in a pillbox. The onslaught was fast and furious, and every man reached for his rifle to fire at the running targets. The Royal Rifles held their section, sweeping the beach with heavy gunfire. Gander stayed close to Fred, who had no choice but to give the dog freedom. There was no time to do anything else. It was now Sergeant Gander's time to prove his reputation as a 'soldier dog'. He didn't have a gun or a bayonet but his sheer size was enough to strike fear into the heart of the advancing army. As the Japanese streamed from their boats and onto the shore, the Canadian forces stood their ground. Rifles raised, they met the challenge of the Imperial Army. Then right in front of Fred and his comrades, Gander rose onto his hind legs. Like a bear, he ran at the Japanese soldiers, baring his teeth. Not even Fred Kelly could stop Gander now. The dog had seen his friends cut down by bombs and now by bullets and bayonets, and his loathing for the Japanese was instantaneous. He stood six foot tall on his hind legs, staring into the stunned faces of the Japanese soldiers as they ran screaming from the dog that they later called the 'Black Devil'.

Fred thought Gander's aggression must have stemmed from the memory of the day they arrived in Kowloon when two Chinese men had tried to abduct him. Until then he had trusted everyone. But that day he learnt there were people to be wary of and the picture he had in his mind matched the look of the soldiers facing his friends right now. For a while Gander waged his own personal war against the Japanese soldiers. If he was afraid, he did not show it. He was fearless and determined to repel the enemy and the Royal Rifles were proud to have him on their side. Time after time he ran in growling at the soldiers, who seemed too shocked to raise their rifles in the attack. Gander was a mascot but at that moment he was a brave soldier too. Gander remained determined to see off the enemy. That he remained alive seemed a miracle, even to the Riflemen serving at his side.

The Royal Rifles gave everything they had to try and stem the flow of the attack. From their slightly elevated position they had a clear view of the enemy and their Bren gun barrels were dangerously hot to the touch from the intense volume of fire. But the invaders kept coming and coming, screeching at the Canadians, with their long bayonets flashing. The Canadians were forced back and 'C' Force was soon in danger of being encircled by the Japanese. Withdrawing southwards to avoid entrapment, the men had another problem – the safe evacuation of the wounded. For those still standing, this was a priority. But by this time the men were also fighting a huge battle against exhaustion. For over a week they had been on continuous front-line duty and the effects of no sleep, no hot food and being constantly under attack were taking their toll on everyone. If they slept at all it would be in a weapon pit or where they collapsed, exhausted, on the roadside. All around, the injured lay amongst the dead, waiting to be taken to safety, but sometimes this could take hours and sitting in an almost constant hail of bullets left them vulnerable.

The remainder of 'C' Force had been forced back down the Lye Mun Road and into the Tai Tam Gap towards the Stanley area. All the time the men were using the sides of the road for shelter from the hail of grenades. The constant Japanese attacks made it difficult for the Royal Rifles to attend to the wounded, who now lay all over the road and in the ditches where they sought shelter. Fred Kelly, like his comrades, was exhausted from the fighting and Gander realized his friend needed his attention now. They lay together in a ditch, but not to rest. From there, Fred noticed another group – this time of wounded Canadians – stranded in the middle of the road. They were about 200 yards away and it looked as if they had been caught in a ferocious exchange of crossfire and were now unable to move in either direction. Then Fred saw Gander standing on the roadside beside them. He had felt the dog move away from him but had not realized where he was going.

'Gander! Get down Gander. Down I said!' Fred Kelly yelled at the dog, afraid that the Japanese would see him first and shoot him. But Gander had already seen his wounded friends and bounded towards them with his usual enthusiasm, only to see several Japanese soldiers moving in fast, their rifles raised in the direction of the wounded. Without hesitating, Gander ran towards them. Growling and baring his teeth, Gander sent them, running and shrieking, in the opposite direction, a look of terror in their eyes. Gander's intervention gave his own men time to recover the wounded without losing ground. It was another brave show by the fearless Canadian dog.

Afraid that Gander would not be so lucky in the next onslaught, Fred took him just a few yards away to one of the pillboxes and secured it as best he could. The pillboxes were still being used as ammunition stores and shelter but most of the action was now being seen on the roadside. 'Now you stay there buddy, until this mess is over … OK? I will come back for you,' Fred said, as he patted Gander's huge head for what he knew could be the last time. Fred was uneasy about leaving Gander this way but he was sure that the dog could not be that lucky again. Why the Japanese didn't shoot him was a real puzzle. As they saw him as the 'Black Devil', maybe they were afraid to do so. No one knows, but it was clear that Gander was lucky to be alive.

Injured soldiers lay everywhere and as the fighting continued through the night, Gander remained on watch. In the early hours of 19 December, the Royal Rifles had begun to make their way into the hills on the south side of Hong Kong Island. Unable to get a clear shot on their target, the Japanese began tossing hand grenades up the hillside towards the men on the off chance they would wound anyone in the vicinity of the blast. But as fast as they were thrown up the hill the Canadians threw them back down before they exploded. And so the lethal game of 'catch' went on.

While the defending Royal Rifles engaged in the dangerous game with the grenades, Captain Garvey and six of his men were making their way into the hills to gain a better view of their target. At this moment a shell hit close by and all seven men were wounded in the blast. Unable to move forward, they immediately became the new target for the Japanese grenades. Blown in several directions by the blast, the men dragged themselves to a point at the side of the road where the captain lay. It was as if the Japanese were watching them, giving them time to move closer together before hitting them with a shower of grenades. One grenade fell just short of the group. One of the men reached for it and tossed it back. Another two grenades landed in the group and were tossed away by the Canadians. Then, as if in slow motion, the men watched a grenade drop into the middle of their group where no one could reach it. The clink of the metal hitting the road seemed to echo for just a moment. Rolling and smoking on the uneven road, the grenade came to a sudden stop. The men quickly located it and every hand moved towards the grenade but all were short. It was just out of reach. Transfixed in their moment of panic and disbelief, they didn't see Gander approaching from behind. No one saw the dog move in. He came from nowhere and, as if he knew what would happen next, he streaked in. Feeling the breeze from the dog's massive body on the move, the men watched in awe as Gander rushed in and picked up the hissing grenade in his mouth. He ran for several yards away from the wounded defending Canadians until the grenade detonated in his mouth, killing him instantly.

The wounded Canadians watched horrified as the grenade exploded. Gander was thrown into the air by the blast. His body lay motionless on the road. Captain Garvey and his men survived and each of them knew they owed their lives to their big black mascot dog.

Gander's body lay on the road all night as the fighting continued. The Canadians fought on to defend their grip on the island and were being pushed back all the time as the grenades continued to be thrown in. No one could reach Gander's body and they had to leave him where he lay. Those who witnessed his bravery had no idea that Fred Kelly was unaware of the dog's death. As far as Fred knew, Gander was in the pillbox where he had left him, away from the fighting. As the news of Gander's bravery made its way through the line, Fred learnt of Gander's heroic deed. The dog had died saving the lives of his friends. Fred had assumed that at the height of the shelling the dog was in the pillbox where he usually slept at night. 'When they started shelling ... I think he must have got scared and ran out of the pillbox,' said Fred later. 'It was pitch dark. I didn't see him run and if I had I would have tried to stop him. But I didn't see him go or save Garvey and his men. That damn dog was a friend to all of us.'

As the sun rose the next morning, the men could see Gander's body still lying on the roadside. It was trapped in the open ground between the two fighting forces where no one could reach him. All the time the men were being forced back by the enemy soldiers, making it impossible to rescue their friend's body. Fred Kelly was Gander's closest friend and the sight of the dog lying dead was more than he could bear. He had served with that dog alongside him since the regiment was stationed at Gander Airfield. They had travelled together the thousands of miles by train and boat to fight on the front line in Hong Kong. They had shared so much together and to have the friendship end this way without a goodbye or being able to bury Gander's body was too painful. 'I think my pals were afraid to tell me that the dog was dead. But I could see that he was dead and I hated that I couldn't go near. To think he was gone hurt me so much and I'm not ashamed to say that I cried. I missed my old pal so much.'

On Christmas Day 1941, Hong Kong was forced to surrender to the Japanese Army. Fred Kelly and his fellow survivors were ordered to come forward and were immediately transported to prisoner of war camps. Those who survived the horror of the camps returned home to Canada but they never forgot their mascot dog, Gander. The men were taken prisoner before they had the chance to collect Gander's body from the roadside where he died. The image of the dog lying there haunted the men for all the time they were prisoners of the Japanese and afterwards in peacetime. They never forgot Gander's bravery and the way he made the ultimate sacrifice for his friends. Those who were saved that cold night in December knew they owed their lives to the dog and they still harboured the hurt they felt when they had to leave him behind.

The exact time of Gander's death is unknown but it's almost certain that his war ended in the early hours of 19 December, within a few hours of the death of another war hero, Sergeant-Major John Osborn. Osborn, an English-born veteran of the First World War, was the first Canadian to receive the Victoria Cross in the Second World War, and it was the only VC awarded for action during the battle for Hong Kong. On the night that Gander saved the lives of seven of his friends in the Royal Rifles of Canada, Sergeant-Major Osborn of the Winnipeg Grenadiers was leading an attack on Mount Butler just a few miles away. Having taken the hill and held it for three hours with only bayonets for weapons, his company was finally forced out by enemy gunfire. Separated from the main battalion, Osborn ignored the rattle of enemy machine guns to gather his men together and lead them to a safer position. When the Japanese began throwing grenades, Osborn began throwing them back. For a while he kept pace with the constant stream of missiles but suddenly one landed too far from his reach. Instinctively, Osborn shouted to warn his men away as he selflessly dived onto the grenade. He was killed instantly but his bravery saved the lives of many others.

Fifty-four years after the fall of Hong Kong a group of veterans were relating the story of Sergeant-Major Osborn to Jeremy Swanson, commemorations officer of the Canadian War Museum. Their memories were to be included in a special exhibition to honour the heroes of the battle in which over 300 Canadians lost their lives and 500 were wounded. The veterans, many of them injured during the fighting for Hong Kong and then held for three years as Japanese prisoners of war, were describing Osborn's selfless act of bravery when one of the men said, 'Yes ... just like that goddam dog!'

It was the start of the conversation that the men had been waiting to have for over half a century. They wanted to relate, not how they had suffered but how a huge, brave Newfoundland dog had saved their lives. They told of the dog's courage and companionship and how they had always wanted a medal for Gander. They wanted the world to know about their gallant mascot.

In Ottawa, Canada, on 27 October 2000, Gander's handler, Fred Kelly, accepted the PDSA Dickin Medal – the medal recognized internationally as the animals' Victoria Cross – on behalf of Gander. The medal is the highest honour any animal can receive for bravery in conflict and it was the day the veteran soldiers and their families had longed for. For Fred Kelly it was, he said, 'the best day of my life!' Gander's Dickin Medal went on to form a proud part of the Canadians' Defence of Hong Kong exhibition at the Canadian War Museum in Ottawa. To the veterans who meet each year to remember friends fallen and heroes lost, Gander is a hero still.

The Hong Kong Veterans Association of Canada (HKVAOC) is still a very active group of veterans and their families, who continue to fight for the recognition of that period of sacrifice. In August 2009 they succeeded in seeing the unveiling of a memorial wall depicting the battle and the names of the people lost in the conflict. The unveiling was a proud and long-awaited moment for the surviving veterans of the Battle of Lye Mun. It was also the foundation stone for the memorial that will go on to feature a bronze of Canada's canine hero – Gander.

During the battle for Hong Kong Gander proved that he was a 'soldier dog'. He was no longer a child's pet, he was a war dog who slept, ate and drank only when he was not facing the enemy. Gander was not trained to be a messenger or a guard dog, like so many other pet dogs were during the Second World War. He just found himself on active service and did what he had done from the start – he gave his friends comfort, companionship and a cosy reminder of home so very far away. But in the throes of battle, Gander was the soldier dog that the hostilities made him.

Gander is now recognized as a Canadian hero of the Second World War. But to his soldier friends he will always be their best pal.

Judy –

Prisoner of War 81A Gloergoer, Medan

'She was in her short lifetime an inspiration of courage, hope and a will to live, to many who would have given up in their time of trial ...'

(Frank Williams, Leading Aircraftsman, RAF)

'Where's Judy? Has anyone seen her?'

British warship HMS *Grasshopper* had been torpedoed. Out of the dark, cold and oily water a sailor shouted to his shipmates in the hope that someone had seen Judy, the ship's mascot. Just moments before the ship was hit, Judy was in her usual place enjoying extra rations in the ship's galley. She belonged to the entire crew and they all looked after her. She was a lucky mascot who, on her previous ship, HMS *Gnat*, had been shelled and almost drowned in the Yangtze River. It seemed Judy was in the wrong place at the wrong time once again.

When Singapore fell to the Japanese in February 1942, *Grasshopper*, a 585-ton river gunboat, left Keppel Harbour in Singapore, bound for Java, her sister ship

HMS *Dragonfly* alongside her. Spotted by a Japanese seaplane both ships were dive bombed. *Grasshopper*, already battle-scarred from the Malaya-Singapore campaign, took a hit under her bow. Commander Hoffman decided to lay-up his ship in a group of islands to the north of Sinkep, but two miles short of safety the ships came under fire again. Two formations of 81 Japanese bombers passed overhead. Nine of the planes at five-minute intervals dropped their bombs and a mile from land the *Grasshopper* was hit astern and set on fire. Many of the 75 crew and 50 passengers (Japanese POWs, Royal Marines, Army officers and civilians) jumped overboard and swam for their lives as the commander beached his ship, which took two more hits before it had to be abandoned.

The survivors, marooned on one of the tiny uninhabited islands in the region, gradually gathered together on the sand. They were in desperate straits. There was very little food to salvage from what was left of the *Grasshopper* and there was no fresh water. Judy had suddenly appeared in the group, much to the relief of the remaining crew. They had lost sight of her in the mayhem of the bombing and assumed she had run for cover in the depths of the ship. Wherever she had been hiding she had, at some stage, made the wise move to head for the water. Weary and covered in oil, the bedraggled dog wandered between the few survivors. The *Grasshopper* and *Dragonfly* had suffered heavy loss of life and those who survived were, like Judy, hungry and thirsty.

The group's priority had been to locate fresh water but for some reason they had not thought to include Judy in their search. After two days, given the poor condition of some of the wounded and the intense heat, the men knew they were on borrowed time and the search for water became desperate. It was one of the ship's crew who noticed Judy sniffing and digging near the shore line. The man drew the others' attention to what Judy was doing and a few of them decided to shadow her. Moving up and down the beach, her nose so close to the sand it was touching her nostrils, Judy detected something. No one was quite sure if she had found something to eat, or uncovered a sea creature, or was just doing what dogs do but they kept an eye on her. Enough of the survivors knew to trust a dog's nose, which was so much more sensitive than any human's. They were right to trust Judy's canine instincts. Two hours later when the tide was out, Judy returned to the chosen spot and started drinking from a spring bubbling up from the sand. Still not sure what the dog was doing, the crew took a closer look. Judy had led the men to a fresh-water spring under the sand. At first no one could believe that the dog had discovered the water, and some were a little unsure if it really was fresh water, but they knew that if they didn't try it they would be dead anyway. Judy was drinking from it and she was fine. Within minutes everyone was crowding around her, scooping up handfuls of the spring water and giving Judy lots of praise. She had saved their lives. And they knew it.

Judy, a pure-bred liver-and-white English pointer, born in Shanghai in 1937 and promptly presented to the Royal Navy as a mascot, had now proven herself to be more than a pet. She was now regarded as a valuable member of the team and was about to start the greatest adventure of her life. Up to this point she had served loyally as a mascot in several ships. She was a survivor and inspired others to aim for the same. Her expertise at finding water had been a godsend. It was several days before the men were presented with the opportunity to commandeer a passing Chinese junk to take them off the island and once again Judy was a ship's mascot, a member of a crew. Respected by all around her, Judy was watched over by the small band of survivors, who regarded her as their guardian angel. Only imagining what lay ahead of them, they knew they just might need that angel again. Filling every container that had washed ashore from the galley with spring water, the men gathered up their mascot dog and boarded the junk.

They set sail for the north-east coast of Sumatra, where they then began a 200-mile trek cross-country to Padang on the west coast of the island, hoping to be able to pick up another boat sailing to India or Ceylon (Sri Lanka) and make their way back to England from there. Walking, hitch-hiking, taking lifts on lorries and river craft, the men made their way. They would only use transport that could take Judy, as there was no way they were going to leave her behind. It was never going to be an easy journey, but having lost every contact possible with the outside world, the *Grasshopper*'s survivors had no idea what was happening around them and, more critically, had no idea of the extent or the position of the Japanese advance. The heat was oppressive and with the water already severely rationed each of the forty or so people walking were on the brink of collapse. No one could gauge how long the water would last out and how far they would have to walk to get to safety. All Commander Hoffman knew was that he had to lead these people to a place of security. They walked with blisters on their feet that they had strapped with strips of their own clothing. They had very little food other than the fruit they knew to be safe off the trees and the generous donations from villages they came across as they trekked on and on through the dense jungle. Each clearing they came to gave rise to very mixed feelings – dread that they were entering enemy territory, or hope that they were safe at last. Village after village emerged out of the undergrowth. It took Commander Hoffman an arduous nine days to get his party within a few miles of Padang. Then, unsuspectingly, their journey almost done, the men stumbled into a Japanese-held village and were immediately taken prisoner. It all happened so quickly. The enemy had probably been watching the group of stragglers for some time before waiting to ambush them as came into the village clearing. With bayonets pointing at their chests and with the sound of Japanese soldiers shrieking orders the survivors of the *Grasshopper* were marshalled into line. It was the beginning of three years of captivity as Japanese prisoners of war in Sumatra – and for Judy too.

Desperate to stay close to the rest of the crew, Judy managed to board the truck bound for the POW camp without being seen. Petty Officer Puncheon grabbed several rice sacks and placed them on top of her, giving her a whispered order to 'stay … still'. The men slipped her water and a little food when they could over the five days it took for them to reach the camp at Rengat. It was here that Leading Aircraftsman Frank Williams set eyes on Judy for the first time. 'I didn't know who she was,' recalled Frank many years later, 'but I remember thinking what on earth is a beautiful English pointer like that doing over here and with no one to care for her. I later learnt that she was a mascot of HMS *Grasshopper* and I realized that even though she looked thin and frail she was a true survivor.'

Frank recognized the same qualities in Judy that he must have recognized in himself, but was far too modest to ever admit. A tall, handsome man with dark wavy hair, a kind face and gentle eyes, at that time untouched by the ravages of years in a prison camp, Frank arrived at Rengat on 13 February 1942 but his journey began weeks before when he was attached to a radar unit operating from a secret location in a rubber plantation in Singapore. The unit received an order to board the SS *Tien Kwong*, a small Royal Navy-operated vessel with small-scale armaments that was tasked with evacuating Service personnel to fight in Java in the event of Singapore falling to the Japanese; and so Frank gathered the valuable radar equipment, destroyed everything else and boarded the boat. The *Tien Kwong* wound its way through the minefields at the entrance to Singapore and into open water. But it didn't take long for Japanese reconnaissance aircraft to pick her up, report her position to the Japanese Air Force and for them to release a squadron of bombers to blow her out of the water.

When the order was given to abandon ship, Frank hoped the bombing had scared the sharks well away as he realized he had a 300-yard swim to shore ahead of him. But the sharks weren't the only danger in these waters. Two other ships, HMS *Kungwo* and HMS *Kuala*, came under Japanese fire. Suddenly the water between ship and shore was alight with burning oil and littered with debris and bodies and people swimming for their lives, as the Japanese planes circled the area releasing their bombs. Many of the passengers on the *Kungwo* were women and children being evacuated from Singapore. Their burnt bodies mingled with those of the military personnel from the other ships.

Frank and his friends tried to get as far away as possible by capturing a local boat and heading for Padang. Picking up supplies of water and coconuts they headed off in their junk. Like the crew of the *Grasshopper*, they hoped to board a ship to India from there. Unfortunately, their craft did not last the distance down the

Indragiri River and had to be abandoned for a truck. By the time they reached Padang, Frank and his friends could go no further. The boat had left for Ceylon and the smaller civilian boats they took from Padang harbour were intercepted by the Japanese. Some did make it to Ceylon but Frank was finally cornered with others planning to escape the grasp of the Japanese. Finally they were rounded up, detained for three months in barracks in Rengat and then transferred north to the POW camp in Medan, where Judy had arrived just days before.

Unsure if anyone had taken the dog under their wing, Frank observed Judy for a while. He saw her wandering and scrounging for food, seemingly half-forgotten and never attached to anyone in particular. Frank remembered first setting eyes on Judy in March 1942 in Rengat; it was now August and he decided he had watched enough of this mournful dog's suffering, and so decided to adopt her. The next afternoon, while the prisoners lined up for their daily ration of rice to be slopped out, Frank decided he would share his with Judy. He took his turn in the queue and headed for his usual place to sit and eat. Judy was around, always, sniffing the ground as she weaved in and out of the crouched figures, heads down and hands in their palm-size bowl, scooping up the grey slop that masqueraded as food. Each person took their ration and, before taking a spoonful, searched through it for signs of life, mainly wriggling maggots. Judy would often move in for the kill when a maggot was flicked to the floor. Making her usual rounds she made her way to Frank's side. Since he arrived, Frank had always been one to save her the odd crumb, so she was used to getting a morsel of food and lots of attention from this fellow prisoner. She eagerly wagged her tail as she swaggered towards him and then did her usual 'sit and stay' pose, which would usually get her a treat. But instead of offering her a grain or two to lick from his fingers, Frank held out the rice bowl. 'Come on Judy … this is yours,' he said. And without hesitation, Judy buried her muzzle into the bowl and lapped up the contents in seconds. Frank held tight to the bowl as Judy licked it cleaner than clean. She nuzzled Frank's arm as if to say, 'Thank you', then lay at his feet and stayed there all day.

After that, Judy followed Frank wherever he went. She continued to share his meagre daily rice ration and gather whatever she could from all over the camp, but she knew she was Frank's dog and it was her job to protect him as much as he was protecting her. And although she regarded Frank as her 'boss', many of the prisoners came to owe their lives to Judy. She had a nose for danger and was quick to warn the men if scorpions, crocodiles, tigers and poisonous snakes were anywhere near. Her most valuable 'gift' was her instinctive dislike of the Korean and Japanese guards. And the feeling was mutual. If any of the men were taken away for a beating, Judy would intervene. Barking, snarling and baring her teeth at the guards she made herself an easy target for a rifle butt in the face. She would start a commotion as soon as the men were presented for public punishment. She would see the gathering of the prisoners, the guards bearing rifles around them and immediately know what was going to happen. Judy then leapt into action, intent on causing a distraction in any way she could. If she was lucky, the end result would be the guards giving up on the beating or the beating being cut short so the guards could chase and punish Judy. Frank would step in to rescue her and haul her back to the hut, where she could remain safe as long as she was confined there for a while and the guards had something else to occupy their time.

Frank knew that the Japanese were not going to tolerate Judy's behaviour for very much longer. He sensed that if he didn't do something drastic to protect his dog, the guards would shoot her. It was a miracle they had not done that so far. The best form of protection Frank could think of was to have Judy officially recognized as a Japanese prisoner of war. He knew that she could not have the full paperwork completed as it would take too long and would involve creating a new POW number. However, choosing a moment when the camp commandant, Colonel Banno, was warm and talkative due to the influence of alcohol, Frank discussed the possibility of Judy sharing his number. This would not have been possible if the colonel had not been so keen on drinking more and more alcohol that night. He was, according to Frank some years later, 'very drunk and seemed to forget that he was speaking to one of the prisoners. I had heard that alcohol put this normally aggressive man in a good mood and given enough to drink he was likely to agree to anything.' The colonel's relationship with Judy was not the friendliest. Judy tolerated the man but would never let him touch her. He often drew his sword and levelled it at her and she would growl in reply. Asking this man to agree to a way that would officially protect Judy from harm was a tall order, but choosing a moment when Banno was drunk was the best time. The warmth of the saki and the promise of one of Judy's puppies for his family secured the agreement. From that night on, Judy was to be listed as: Prisoner of War 81A Gloergoer, Medan. She was the only dog to be officially recognized as a POW and for that protection she owed her life to Frank Williams.

There was little time or opportunity for Judy to socialize with other dogs but there was evidence that she had at least one male friend when she gave birth to a litter of seven puppies. The father was thought to be a gutsy little mongrel from the adjoining village that visited the camp regularly enough to earn himself a name – Tich. The happy-go-lucky dog was a welcome visitor to the prisoners but no dog was a favourite with the guards. One evening, as Frank was getting water for the hut he saw one of the guards raise his rifle above what looked like a grey, shadowy mass on the ground. There was something odd about what he was looking at. Someone was going to be hurt and Frank could not stop himself moving closer to the fence to see what was happening. Suddenly, Frank heard a blood-curdling yelp as he saw the rifle hit with a thud. Unable to hold back, Frank pushed through the wire, over to where the guard was still standing with his rifle over his head. The grey shadow at his feet was a dog. It was Tich. The guard had broken his neck. That was too much for Frank to bear. Elbowing the guard out of the way, Frank leant down to the frail body on the ground and cradled the dog's head in his hands. He could not save Tich. He was too late on the scene.

What Frank didn't know at that time was that Judy had heard the commotion and was heading to join him by the perimeter fence. Fortunately, she was in the hut and the other prisoners would not let her out. They were always afraid to let her wander if Frank wasn't there. She could hear Tich in distress and she must have wanted to be with him very much. As she scratched at the hut door, her fellow prisoners held her back. Part of them probably wanted to let her go but everyone knew that if she had made it to the fence and appeared in front of that guard she would have been killed too.

Taking on the guards was never a wise move, everyone knew that, but at the moment Frank leapt to Tich's side it could not have been further from his mind. Now, however, Frank awaited punishment for attempted escape. The reason why he had gone through the fence and the fact that he had not made any attempt to escape was immaterial in the camp. No one wanted to hear about Tich. No one wanted to know why Frank was angry. As far as his captors were concerned, Frank was guilty and punishment was due – eight hours of beatings by two guards. This was not an uncommon punishment and Judy sensed what was going on. She had seen this happen too many times and there was only one way to keep her from running to Frank's aid. Judy had to be locked away for her own safety. If she had intervened it would have been the excuse the guards were no doubt waiting for to beat her too – or worse.

In this harsh environment the prisoners tried hard to enjoy any small feelings of normality. Having Judy around made this almost possible and when she gave birth to her litter of puppies, it became a community event. It was a wise move to present the commandant, Colonel Banno, with one of the puppies. It was one thing he remembered from the night when Frank persuaded him to list Judy as a POW. But instead of taking the puppy to his family he gave little Kish to his lady friend as a gift. Another puppy, Sheikje, was smuggled by a fruit seller into the Dutch women's camp in Medan and Rokok was given a whiff of chloroform to smuggle him to the Swiss Consul through a small drain hole in the compound wall. Punch became a camp dog, running between everyone and begging where he could. The remainder of the litter were less fortunate. They were discovered by the guards and despatched with bullets from a rifle when they were just a few days old. The only consolation being, it was a quick death.

By June 1944 Colonel Banno was transferred out of the camp. He had completed his time there and word was that he had been sent on active service in Malaya. The new commandant, Captain Nishi, was a small man with a huge capacity for cruelty and Judy loathed him on sight. Just one look from him, with his deep-set black eyes and pitted face, and she would growl and bare her teeth until he moved away or Frank called her off. Colonel Banno had been a tough disciplinarian but he had not targeted Judy for any punishment, even though he could have. Nishi was very different. He was very keen on dealing out beatings for no apparent reason and he was a dog hater to boot. It was no wonder that Frank sensed that Judy was in constant danger with Captain Nishi in charge.

Not long after his arrival Nishi made an announcement: the prisoners were to be transferred to another camp, this time in Singapore. The thought of being away from Nishi's gaze was a huge relief for Frank but the celebration was short-lived. Nishi ordered the prisoners to prepare to leave the following day but that NO DOG was to travel with them.

Frank Williams had not come this far to leave his faithful companion behind. As the others made their preparations to board the merchant ship SS *Van Warwyck* the next day, Frank had to find a way of making sure Judy made the journey safely to Singapore. It was a plan that was going to take all night to work out and one that could only succeed if it held up to the guards' scrutiny. If Judy was discovered she would be shot and most likely Frank too. The plan had to be good.

His first thought was to put Judy in a small brown trunk that a Dutch prisoner found from somewhere in the camp. But the trunk was bound to be hauled over for inspection and everyone, not just Frank, would be in trouble for defying Nishi's orders. However, if there was one thing more commonplace than maggots in the rice rations it was rice sacks. And that gave Frank an idea. From dusk until dawn Frank coached Judy in getting in and out of a rice sack in double-quick time and then being slung over his shoulder. At first light the prisoners were lined up and counted.

In accordance with Captain Nishi's orders, Frank had tied Judy to a post outside their hut. After checking the loose slipknot in her rope and telling her to 'sit and stay' he went to join the others. He could tell Judy was confused but she didn't make a fuss and Frank prayed that she would sit still for as long as he needed her to. The commandant checked that his orders had been carried out and the men could see he was pleased with the result. He dared not touch Judy, as she sat patiently by the hut, but she played her part well and as the men turned out of the gates of the camp, Frank whistled softly to Judy, who slipped her rope and scampered towards him. Nishi was already celebrating his victory over the dog and her fellow prisoners and didn't see Judy's timely escape.

Slinking away through the gate, nestled in between the legs of the prisoners as they marched out of the compound, Judy kept up with the men. They were heading for a train just ahead of the camp gates so it would be easier if Judy was in a sack as soon as possible. At the first opportunity, Frank opened the rice sack as a colleague lifted the dog inside, and they boarded the train that was waiting to take them to the docks. As soon as they arrived there, Judy was emptied from the sack and told to stay close to the train for cover, as it was where the men were told to wait too. It was almost impossible to expect Judy to understand the new rules and new environment but it was her task to stay far enough away from Frank not to be seen by the guards and close enough to be lifted into a rice sack at a moment's notice.

Lined up on the station platform it was time for another inspection ahead of the men boarding the ship for the next leg of their journey. This time the guards seemed more interested in inspecting the bundles and pack sacks lying on the ground, and parcels were ordered to be opened and then checked a second time. Frank's rice sack lay at his feet. Judy was poised and waiting to hear Frank's soft whistle. At the right moment, he bent down, opened the end of the sack, gave a low whistle and Judy moved stealthily between the lines towards Frank. A friend then lifted Judy into the sack and slung it over Frank's shoulder. Frank knew he was being watched very closely and every time he saw a guard lunge a bayonet at a prisoner's bag of belongings he held his breath. He knew the guards had seen Judy left behind but he also knew the Japanese were suspicious. He wasn't surprised to be challenged by one of the camp guards asking, 'Dog not come?' Frank and everyone around him just shrugged their shoulders.

For the next two hours the men were forced to stand on parade, motionless in the blazing tropical sun. Judy was upside down in the rice sack the whole time. She didn't whimper and hardly took a breath. She was so still that at one stage Frank thought she had died from heat exhaustion. She just knew what she had to do and Frank trusted her. It was a huge thing to ask a dog to do and an incredible physical feat to be able to manage what Judy did that day. She did it for Frank and he did not let her down. As fellow prisoners collapsed in the heat, Frank knew he could not do that. He had Judy to protect.

The heat was stifling and seemingly relentless. For Frank the focus was on staying upright, and as soon as the men were allowed on board the *Van Warwyck*, an ancient Dutch tramp steamer, Judy was safely released into the boat's hold where she slept at Frank's feet.

Over 700 men were crammed below the rusted deck in the dark and subjected to the unbearable heat. Tiers and tiers of wooden platforms provided space for the men to lie, like sardines, as the boat steamed at pedestrian speed off the coast of Sumatra. Above deck the Japanese crew had stacked machinery and bales of rubber they had looted from local factories and workshops.

Judy was born into the muggy heat of the Far East but the heat on this journey was overwhelming. Frank was afraid Judy would be ill and he wouldn't be able to get help for her as she was still in hiding from the guards. So on the second day man and dog went on the move. Frank remembered a corner on the top tier of the platforms near the bulkhead, where he had hidden with Judy the day before so the guards would not see her through the hatch. He decided to make his way back there with two of his friends, knowing they couldn't be seen from any angle as they sat with their backs to the bulkhead. It was a relief to have a few inches of headroom and for Judy it was heaven to have a 10-inch porthole to peep out of. As the constant thud of the ship's engines lulled everyone into a sense of calm, Judy rested her head on Frank Williams's legs and slept the hours away.

A day later, 26 June 1944, as the boat made its way through the muddy depths of the Malacca Straits, the stillness was broken by the crack of a torpedo hitting the steamer. The explosion lit up the sky and a billowing cloud of smoke poured out of the depths of the boat. The air was thick with oily dust and in the pitch black of the hold there was a smouldering mess of twisted metal and splintered timber. In the confusion Frank briefly lost sight of Judy but she soon found him and nuzzled her nose into his chest just to remind him that she wasn't going anywhere without him. But the *Van Warwyck* was filling with water and listing badly. Judy and her fellow survivors had little time to escape. Suddenly the 10-inch porthole looked like the ideal escape route for one of the prisoners. Frank knew it would be impossible to carry Judy through the wreckage to safety, and he was not going to leave her behind, so there was only one thing for it – Judy was going through the porthole. Opening the gap as wide as possible Frank was hopeful that his plan would work, although it had to be done quickly.

Lifting Judy and easing her head and front legs through the opening, he gave the dog her orders: 'Now old girl, when I push you through you must swim. Do you hear me?' Judy gave Frank one of her normal mournful glances, although she must have understood because the look she gave her master was enough to say, 'Well, I hear you but I still think you are crazy!' Folding Judy's back legs underneath her body and trying his best to protect her body as it passed through the gap, Frank pushed Judy out. It was a 15-foot drop to the water. He had no idea if she would survive the fall but he knew that she would not survive the scramble through the burning debris that now faced him and his friends. Knowing instinctively that he would see Judy again, Frank made good his escape.

In panic and in the half light survivors used the crates and packing cases floating through the boat to climb up and out of the hold. They knew that if they stayed longer in the wreck it would explode, taking them with it. As the crew and prisoners emerged onto the deck they were faced with the fast-flowing current and the flash of two more torpedoes exploding near to the wrecked *Van Warwyck*. The old steamer was going down fast and the men had to swim as far away as possible to avoid being sucked down with it. Quickly, Frank studied the floating debris. He scanned the surface and then looked deeper into the water. There was no sign of Judy. He looked desperately for a glimpse of her but there was nothing and he had to get into the water. He slid down the barnacle-encrusted hull and lowered himself into the black swill, still looking for Judy. He didn't take his eyes off the water as he hurried as best he could to get clear of the sinking ship. Briefly turning onto his back, Frank saw a massive column of water erupting from the old steamer. Her boilers had ruptured and she made her final decent beneath the water.

For over two hours Frank swam in the oily debris-strewn sea looking for Judy, but there was no trace of her. He started to ask around to see if anyone else in the water had seen her. Even if they had seen her dead body, at least he would have known her fate. Many of those who had survived the sinking of the SS *Van Warwyck* and her three escort boats were clinging onto whatever object they could find just to survive. A dog in all that mayhem was hardly going to be noticed – and Frank knew that. But he was about to find out that Judy was not only alive, she was saving people's lives by letting them cling to her as she guided them to safety.

When Frank heard about this wonderful dog, he knew it had to be Judy. He had spent the previous three days on a tanker that had moved in to pick up the survivors, and all that time he had been asking about Judy. Had anyone seen her? He discovered that he was surrounded by people who had seen Judy and even some that had been saved by her, but no one could say where she was now. Thoughts of her being alone without any protection from the fierce daytime sun and the freezing temperatures at night began to play on Frank's mind until he was convinced that he would never see Judy again. He wondered how she could survive when she must be so weak. She had been in the water for hours and used her strength helping others. Surely it had all been too much for the old girl?

When the tanker dropped its cargo of bedraggled POWs in Singapore, the dockyard bristled with German U-boats. The men stretchered their wounded to the trucks that were waiting to take them to their new camp and as he staggered along with his fellow survivors, Frank was more than convinced that one or more of the U-boats tied up alongside the dock was responsible for firing the torpedoes that sent the tramp steamer to the bottom of the Malacca Straits. Convinced that Judy had perished when the submarines had attacked, Frank's anger and despondency grew by the second. Frank lost many friends that day and the thought of losing Judy was unbearable.

As the truck pulled up outside the gates of the new camp, Frank looked back behind him, just in case Judy had landed ashore after all and had followed on. But the road was clear of everything but vehicles transporting prisoners and lorries full of furniture and other rich pickings looted from the homes of the foreign residents. Stepping off the tailgate to line up for one more roll-call Frank saw something in the corner of his eye. He wanted it to be Judy. So many nights now he had prayed that Judy would just walk back into his life as she had done before. She seemed to just turn up. 'I couldn't believe my eyes. As I entered the camp a scraggy dog hit me square between the shoulders and knocked me over! Coated in bunker oil, her tired old eyes were burned red. Judy! I'd never been so glad to see the old girl. And I think she felt the same about me!' The reunion of man and dog was joyous and touching.

The 'old girl' had reached the camp well ahead of Frank, thanks to a fellow prisoner who had plucked her out of the sea and helped her aboard a small boat sent to collect the wounded. Her rescuer had kept her hidden under the folds of a black cloth draped over a table where a dead Korean guard had been laid out. When she jumped ashore in Singapore Judy became part of the convoy being taken to River Valley Camp in Singapore, and as she was being hoisted aboard a transport truck Judy was spotted by her nemesis – Captain Nishi. He had travelled with the rest of the camp guards and was on duty that day on the dockside. He was furious to see Judy alive and, in his eyes, the prisoners had made him look a fool in front of his men. Here was the dog that was supposed to have been left behind. Left for dead. Filled with anger he ordered the guards to throw the dog into the sea. But as they approached her a loud voice issued a command that stopped everyone in their tracks. The voice belonged to Colonel Banno, who had heard of the sinking and had hurried to the docks. It was this dog's lucky day and she spent it on a truck with her companions bound for the new camp.

After just a month in Singapore, the prisoners were shipped back to Sumatra. The men were needed as a workforce to complete the construction of a railway through the central Sumatran jungle. A paddle steamer stood ready to take them on the two-day journey to their destination and once again Judy had to be smuggled aboard. This time she knew exactly what to do as Frank and his friends made sure she was kept well out of the guards' sight.

For the next year the prisoners moved from camp to camp, laying miles and miles of rail track, all the time cutting through swathes of dense undergrowth. For hours and hours each day they worked in the relentless heat and with very little food or water. The sick and the dying were not spared from the work and were beaten severely if they fell behind with their tasks. The prisoners were at risk of falling victim to any of the many diseases that spelt almost certain death in the jungle. Dysentery, malaria, cholera and beriberi were rife and often fatal, especially when combined with the greatest killer of them all – starvation. Frank and Judy survived on the daily ration of a handful of boiled rice, which they shared equally and with relish, no matter how many maggots or insects were crawling around in it. Many men died where they dropped amongst the jungle green and their friends were forced to move on without them unless they could quickly construct a makeshift stretcher. They would do this even though they didn't have the strength to carry another human being, even one that was little more than a walking skeleton.

Frank lived in fear of developing beriberi. He had overcome black water fever, cholera and several attacks of malaria but beriberi couldn't be beaten without medical attention and good food, neither of which was available to the jungle POWs. Without these necessities life expectancy was three to four months at most, and the survivors had seen it all often enough. They knew that once the ankles started to swell, heart failure and death would follow. 'It was the depression that was hard to fight off,' said Frank, later. 'We all knew that swollen ankles indicated the beginning of the end and the real battle then was to keep the depression at bay. Once that got hold of you, death was certain. Sometimes it was easier to make up excuses for not wanting to stay alive. Every day I thanked God for Judy. She saved my life in so many ways. The greatest way of all was giving me a reason to live.'

It seemed to Frank that Judy could read him like a book: 'All I had to do was look at her and into those weary, bloodshot eyes and I would ask myself: What would happen to her if I died? I thought of her crawling into the jungle to die alone of starvation and it was an unbearable thought. We had been through too much together and I knew in an instant that I couldn't let that happen. I had to keep going for her. Even if it meant waiting for a miracle.'

The jungle was a harsh and hostile place where Judy suffered the same deprivations as the men. She became a different dog to the docile ship's mascot Frank saved from starvation almost three years before. Judy the POW was a lean and wily animal who relied on cunning and raw instinct for survival.

While the men were laying over 3,000 miles of jungle railway for the Japanese, Judy devoted her time to supplementing her diet of maggot-ridden rice with anything she could run fast enough to catch and eat from her jungle larder. Snakes, rats, monkeys and lizards became tasty meals to this starving dog and the game of catching them seemed to give her just as much pleasure as eating them. Hunger often made her brave and Frank was always afraid that her habit of teasing the fierce Sumatran tigers would, one day, lead to bloodshed. The day she decided to challenge a crocodile was the day she discovered that she could not catch and eat everything. Frank saw the tear in his dog's side and knew that something much larger than another dog had attacked her. A fellow prisoner recognized the bite marks and confirmed that Judy had taken on a crocodile. It left a huge scar on her side to remind her that she was not invincible.

It was her brave and constant attacks on the guards that finally resulted in Judy being condemned to death. Beatings were a daily part of camp life and Judy couldn't bear it. As soon as she saw a prisoner being tied and ordered on to their knees, she would rush in barking and snarling at the guards as they dealt out the punishment. Judy's interference would inevitably cause a disruption and each time it happened Frank thought Judy would be shot before he could drag her out of trouble. For some reason, it never happened. But it was the day Frank took a beating that Judy's life was put in the greatest danger.

There never appeared to be a reason for the beatings but they were a constant reminder, if any was needed, that the guards were in charge. However, when Judy saw the guard raise his whip to Frank, she could not be held back. There was a huge scuffle as the guard shouted for reinforcements, who battled to regain control of the situation. The commandant heard the commotion from his office and emerged to control the situation. He ordered the dog to be detained and he issued a final warning to the men: if Judy was seen on the camp again she would be shot and fed, as meat, to the prisoners.

Judy was already living a nomad's life between the camp and the jungle. It wasn't safe for her to be in the camp all the time and it wasn't safe to be in the jungle either. She still regarded herself as Frank's dog, and everyone knew that, but he had to insist that she sought safety in the jungle when necessary. With the 'wrong' guard on duty, her life would be at risk. She was going to have to spend the majority of time in the jungle now for her own safety, and the range of whistled communications that Frank and Judy had developed between them over the years would now come into its own. During the day she stayed deep in the undergrowth well out of sight of the guards: at night, but only on Frank's strict instruction, was she allowed into the camp for some much-missed fuss and attention. On hearing a low whistle from Frank, Judy would stealthily make her way from her hiding place across to the fence and through the gap into the camp. It was the only way to assure her safety and Frank was in no doubt that the guards would carry out their threat. She had enjoyed many lucky escapes to date, but it was only a matter of time before her luck ran out.

No one wanted that to happen. It was her grit and determination that inspired everyone around her. She stood up to the guards in the camp, the tigers and crocodiles in the jungle, and she battled with starvation and disease. The men met the same challenges but not all of them survived. Judy was often in the wrong place at the wrong time but she came through and she did that with Frank at her side. Survival wasn't her only skill. Judy was a POW but she was also a dog, and her canine antics were often the source of much-needed laughter. Seeing Judy chase monkeys and flying foxes was sheer entertainment but, for the prisoners, her finest moment was the time she found an elephant's shin bone and then spent the rest of the day trying to bury it!

The men had been subjected to a living hell laying rail track that would be overgrown before it was used, and had seen their fellow prisoners fall in their hundreds due to exhaustion and disease. To them, Judy was a sane link with home comfort and normality. She gave the men hope when it was in short supply and many were reported to have said, in the darkest times of fear and despair, 'If the old bitch can hang on for release, then I can make it too!'

By August 1945 food suddenly became more plentiful in the camp and rumours about a Japanese surrender were rife. While the men were working deep in the jungle had peace been declared? When the commandant gathered the prisoners together and announced that the war was over it was hard for the men to believe. The torture was over. They were no longer prisoners of war. And that included Judy. 'Hey you know something Judy? Now this horrid war is over you can have your own rice ration. There'll be no need to share with me!' said Frank. For Frank and his fellow prisoners their first thought was to reach for a rifle and subject the guards to the kind of punishment they had been dealing out in the camp, but they didn't get the chance. Within hours of the announcement the guards had fled.

Over the next few days the prisoners had a chance for the idea of freedom to sink in, and the appearance of the RAF Liberator aircraft helped the dream take form in reality as they carried in men and much-needed rations. Parachutes rained from the sky carrying relief supplies. The food and the Allied soldiers were a comforting sight to men who had spent three years fighting disease and starvation at the hands of their captors. As a tribute to the prisoners a visit from Admiral Lord Louis Mountbatten – Supreme Allied Commander of South East Asia – and Lady Edwina Mountbatten was arranged and it proved both a proud and surreal moment. The visitors looked so overly elegant and highly polished standing next to the former prisoners, who looked like nothing more than skeletons in rags. And Judy stood with them sharing the moment. Since joining the Royal Navy she had known little but being bombed, shot at and almost drowned. In the camps she shared rations, dodged disease and eked out life in a place where death surrounded her. If only she knew that her hope and faith had paid off. It was time to go home.

Leaving the steamy jungles of Sumatra for the civilization of Singapore, the prisoners were immediately transferred to hospital where a health assessment was carried out and every man was given the chance to rest and eat under medical supervision. Many of the ex-Sumatran prisoners needed more than the four weeks allotted for recuperation and some were so seriously ill that they were immediately flown back to Britain for specialist care. Frank's time in hospital, with Judy beside him, was spent thinking about taking Judy home to meet his parents and his sister. As a borderline health case he was high on the list for an immediate flight home, but he needed more time to secure Judy's passage home so they would not be parted again. Frank had to talk quickly to those in charge and have his name removed from the passenger list, knowing that his failure would result in Judy being abandoned to an uncertain fate in Singapore – and that simply wasn't going to happen.

Despite his desperate pleas for more time, Frank only gained a two-day respite before finding himself on a truck heading for Singapore docks and the troopship SS *Antenor.* The ship was bound for Liverpool but from the moment he and Judy arrived on the dockside there was a problem. Frank was met by something he really didn't expect – a notice forbidding animals aboard the ship. The gangway was heavily guarded and Frank knew at a glance that the only way he was going to get Judy aboard was to smuggle her one last time.

The plan was simple: Judy stayed on the dockside as Frank and his friends filed up the gangway, spacing themselves out as they went. It was then up to a couple of the men to create a disturbance and, while the patrol guards were distracted, Frank gave a low whistle to Judy, who then made her way onto the ship where Frank was waiting to intercept her. Then man and dog disappeared below deck. Judy was safely hidden below Frank's bunk until they were in open water – just to be sure. If she had been discovered before then there was no doubt at all that Judy would have not made the trip to England. It would have broken Frank's heart.

It was three days before Judy was discovered by the authorities on board and by that time no one cared about a skinny dog or the fact that she was a stowaway. There was only one thing on everyone's mind – getting home. To see the old girl have her freedom was a necessity. No one could bear to see the dog that had been their companion and best friend suffer any more. After years of virtual starvation and days filled with fear Judy and Frank were now safe, and thanks to the fact the *Antenor*'s cook was a dog lover, Judy was assured all the food she could eat – and more.

Judy's favourite haunt was the galley but she was used to a life where she could wander between her friends in the camp and her jungle hideaway, so it was difficult for Frank to deny the dog her desire to roam. Everywhere she went on the ship the men and crew were surprised to see this fairly large dog scampering along the deck. They were even more surprised to hear her story and over the 10 weeks it took the troopship to reach Liverpool, admiration for the brave POW dog that kept morale and men alive in the camp grew and grew. When Frank was told that it might not be possible for Judy to leave the ship when it reached port, the swell of disapproval towards the authorities was overwhelming. Judy had come so far with the men no one was going to abandon her now.

A flurry of messages was telegraphed to London seeking permission for Judy to disembark in England. The father of a fellow RAF prisoner of war finally secured the arrangements for Judy's landing in Liverpool and a wave of relief was felt throughout the ship. As they docked in Liverpool Judy looked to Frank for her next instruction. Frank knew that the quarantine officials would be waiting to take Judy from him so she could begin her six months in the government kennels in Surrey but there was one place he wanted his dog to go before she began her 'sentence', and that was to the NAAFI canteen and its Aladdin's cave of good things to eat. For a dog used to a diet of mouldy rice she took immediately to a heap of cream buns set out on a plate on the counter. Judy had never seen a cream bun in her life but managed to demolish several before being taken away. She looked at Frank to make sure that he really meant to tell her to 'go'. Her tail was wagging but Frank sensed her reluctance, and he reassured her that, this time, she had to leave her master behind.

It was a week before Frank saw Judy again and the meeting was emotional. Frank kept his promise to Judy to visit her as often as he could and it helped pass the long hours spent alone in her quarantine kennel. Ironically, even as a POW she had never spent that much time under lock and key. She had also never been alone before, as Frank and his fellow prisoners had always kept her company and kept her safe no matter if she was in the camp or the jungle. When she eventually decided to eat what was offered at mealtimes in the kennels, Judy began to slowly put on weight and when her six months were up she emerged a strong, healthy dog. Only her oh-so-sad eyes gave any clue to all that she had suffered in her war.

Frank was not the only person waiting for Judy's release from quarantine. The world's press had heard the good news that the only dog to be officially registered as a prisoner of war was to receive the animal kingdom's highest award for bravery in conflict – the PDSA Dickin Medal – in recognition of her life-saving devotion to Frank and the other prisoners. Frank also received the charity's White Cross of St Giles in recognition of his determination to protect Judy from harm. The presentation of the medals was made at the

Returned Prisoner of War Association headquarters in London, and in his address to the assembled company the Chairman of the Association, Viscount Tarbat, referred to Judy's determination to protect Frank and their fellow prisoners. Many of the men owed their life to Judy, not only because she may have saved them from a snake bite or a scorpion's sting or a beating at the hands of the camp guards but because she gave them the inspiration to survive. Frank Williams said many times that he owed his life to the 'old girl'. Judy's PDSA Dickin Medal citation reads:

For magnificent courage and endurance in Japanese prison camps, which helped maintain morale among her fellow prisoners and also for saving many lives through her intelligence and watchfulness.

For many other dogs that would be the end of the story, but not for Judy – or Frank Williams. The BBC's Victory Day broadcast on 8 June 1946 included Judy as special guest and her bark was heard all over the world. It was heard as far as Singapore and all points north, south, east and west. Once again she made canine history – this time by being the first dog to bark on air. After attending a special parade of war dogs and Victoria Cross recipients at the Dorchester Hotel, Frank and Judy established themselves as celebrities and helped raise many thousands of pounds for the PDSA and children's charities all over the United Kingdom. They were a working partnership and adored by the media the world over.

As a Royal Air Force mascot (having given up her career as a Royal Navy mascot when Frank adopted her) Judy was presented with a special coat to wear on ceremonial occasions while she was stationed at air bases in Sunninghill Park in Berkshire and Cosford in Shropshire. But the publicity Judy gained for her bravery as a prisoner of war had a deep affect on the families who had lost loved ones in the prison camps. Thousands of letters poured in for Frank's attention and almost all of them wanted to know what had happened to their relative out there in the jungle. The black-edged telegram sent by the military was not enough for many. They wanted to know what their loved one would have gone through on a daily basis and how they could have succumbed to the enemy in the end. So Frank and Judy took to the road visiting bereaved families, bringing knowledge and peace where possible. 'Judy always seemed to cushion the news we carried,' wrote Frank later. 'Her presence comforted many who up to that time had lived many anxious months and years of uncertainty without knowing the truth.'

On 22 July 1946 Frank Williams and Judy were demobbed from the RAF. Even on her last day Judy wore her large leather collar that bore a silver plate inscribed with the name of every area of conflict she had been involved in, alongside her campaign medal ribbons. It was the end of the chapter as far as Judy's wartime career was concerned but not the end of her life as a faithful hero dog. That chapter was just about to begin.

Frank Williams was not a man to settle to domesticity. No one knew if the war had made him an adventurer and captivity had given him a thirst for living life freely and to the full, but wherever he travelled and whatever job he chose to do Judy was to be his loyal companion. In 1948 the lure of a government-funded food scheme in East Africa sent Frank and Judy back overseas. This time Frank hoped there would be no need to smuggle Judy anywhere but from the moment they reached the airport Frank hit his first bureau-cratic hitch when he was told that Judy could not fly on the same plane. Appealing to his old friends at PDSA and the Returned Prisoner of War Association, Frank managed to run rings round the officials and Judy took her seat next to Frank as they headed for East Africa.

Based in what is now Tanzania, Judy was at home with the wide variety of wildlife that surrounded Frank's home. In many ways it was like being back in the jungle for Judy except that this time she had the chance to chase ostrich and giraffe too. Judy never forgot the law of the jungle and that was to stand her in good stead in the African bush. Many times she protected Frank and his African servants, Adolf and Abdul his driver, from poisonous snakes and insects. Judy always sought them out and disposed of them first. Chasing baboons became her favourite pastime although they often had the last laugh. By throwing sticks and corn cobs at Judy they always won, but Judy didn't mind.

There was one fascination she transferred with her from Sumatra, and that was to do with elephants. Frank said they intrigued her because she couldn't work out which end was which! When one crept into the camp one night to drink Frank's discarded bath water, Judy decided to stalk it in true English pointer style. When Frank came out of the hut to see what was making the horrendous slurping noises, he saw Judy striking a perfect and defiant pointer pose in the face of an immovable and very thirsty bull elephant.

For two years Judy enjoyed life in Africa and sharing in Frank's work and travels. Everyone came to know the man with the dog and once again Judy gained her own brand of celebrity status. She even managed to find time to give birth to a litter of nine puppies. Frank's work often took him away from his base camp and wherever he went Judy would always go along for the ride. But a routine visit to a stretch of land 14 miles from his base in Nachingwea went horribly wrong. It wasn't unusual for Judy to go on her own hunting trip while Frank went about his work but this time she didn't return. Abdul and Adolf joined Frank in the search, which went on well into the darkness but she was nowhere to be found. Judy had disappeared without a trace.

Frank wasted no time in posting notices in and around the place she had gone missing and he offered a reward of 100 shillings for her safe return. Accompanied by an experienced tracker, Frank searched the area for days, crossing swamps and flooded rivers and following tracks and trails deep into the bush. On the fifth day of Judy's disappearance they came upon a bamboo hut where an elder of the village sat outside smoking his pipe. The old man gave his name as Heneko, a member of the Mbwa tribe, and he told them how he had seen a strange-looking brown and white dog in the neighbouring village about 12 hours earlier. Frank decided to walk there himself in the hope that even if she had moved on she might go back there for food, as there was nothing else for miles. He left, asking Heneko to watch for her as he would come back that way. Judy did not return.

On the eighth day since Judy's disappearance, Heneko met with Frank again. This time there was a positive sighting of Judy in another village and a search party was quickly arranged for the morning. It was agreed that if anyone found her they must hold her in one of the huts and inform Frank right away. The villagers remembered seeing Judy and they knew she wanted food, but many of them were too afraid of the 'big dog' and she was made to leave. Often she was mistaken for a lioness searching for food and they were afraid of her. This was probably why she had wandered so far from her starting point. Thankfully Judy did return to the village in search of food and this time the villagers were able to detain her until Frank arrived the next morning.

Frank had not seen Judy so thin and weak since their days in the prison camp in Sumatra. She was ridden with parasites eating her flesh, and cuts and bruises covered her body. Her sunken sides were pitiful and the sight of her looking so ill and weak made Frank cry like he never thought he could. She had not eaten for some time but she still managed to wag her tail even if she couldn't walk across the room to greet him. Frank paid the villagers the reward money and hurried to get back to Nachingwea. Judy needed to be protected from the tsetse flies, and the cattle ticks that covered her body had to be removed immediately as she had already lost a huge amount of blood. When they eventually arrived back at Frank's base camp Judy gulped down a plate of chicken with milk. A warm bath with disinfectant removed the remaining cattle ticks and made her more comfortable and she was able to rest for the first time in days. She was safe. Twelve hours of dream-filled sleep followed, with Frank watching every breath and every jerk of her body. The old girl had cheated death again.

After a few days of Frank's tender care Judy started to show a glimmer of her lively old self. But the recovery was short-lived. She had always been prone to mammary tumours and during the time she was lost in the bush another growth had developed rapidly. The problem was that Judy was too weak to undergo the essential surgery to remove it, but if the tumour burst she would have no chance of survival. Dr Gordon, Frank's trusted vet, was familiar with Judy's condition and all that she had suffered before her move to Africa. He told Frank that it was a gamble he should take. Judy might not be strong enough to pull through the anaesthetic, but without the surgery she would die anyway. This dog had been through so much she deserved the best possible chance.

The operation was a complete success and after two days Judy looked as if she was going make a complete recovery. But her time in the bush had taken its toll on her weakened body and although she rallied round in typical style she was clearly in some pain. It was down to Frank to make the final decision for his beloved companion.

On 17 February 1950 Judy was put peacefully to sleep. Frank could not bear to see her suffer after all that she had lived through and all that she had done for him. She was 13 years old; a good age for a dog who had been through so much and cheated death a million times over. Frank wrapped Judy in her RAF service coat and placed her carefully in a box. He buried her in a clearing not far from his hut and covered the place with stones to stop the hyenas disturbing it. For more than two months Abdul and Adolf helped Frank gather pieces of white marble in the bush until they had enough to put round the three-ton concrete block that was to form Judy's tombstone over her grave. The metal plaque that was attached to the stone told the story of a brave dog. In Frank's words:

> a remarkable canine ... a gallant old girl who with a wagging tail gave more in companionship than she ever received ... and was in her short lifetime an inspiration of courage, hope and a will to live, to many who would have given up in their time of trial had it not been for her example and fortitude ...

Rest in peace ... Prisoner of War 81A Gloergoer, Medan.

It was Frank Williams's wish that after his death, Judy's collar and her animals' VC be presented to the Imperial War Museum in London for safekeeping. In April 2004 Frank's family travelled from their home in

British Columbia, Canada to present the items to the Director General of the Museum and to request that Judy's story be kept alive for many generations to share and enjoy.

Caesar –

A Digger
and a Dog

'He was a mongrel from death row. He was
saved and conscripted to serve his country.
He asked for nothing but we asked him to give
everything. To the soldier, the Vietnam War
was like all wars – about mateship and loss.'

(Peter Haran, Vietnam War veteran, handler of
Australian Tracker dog, Caesar, and author of *Trackers:
The Untold Story of the Australian Dogs of War*)

They say you should never go back. But I guess that depends on what you've left behind. For Vietnam War veteran Peter Haran it was the memory of touching death every day, the bond shared with men who lived the same nightmares and, above all, an irrepressible love for a dog called Caesar.

On 16 February 2008 Peter joined fellow veterans of the Australian Forces to pay their respects to the men who had fought and died in the war in Vietnam, from 1966 to 1972. It was a scorching day, reminiscent of the many days he had spent not yards from the same spot as a young digger (soldier) at the Australian Task Force base at Nui Dat, southern Vietnam. An old soldier recounts the events of 21 July 1969, the day man first walked on the moon, the day a young lieutenant walked over an M16 'jumping jack' mine, blowing away his leg and sending deadly fragments of metal searing into the 30-man-strong platoon. This was the spot. This was his memory. These were the tears fought back for almost forty years. For Peter Haran the journey back and the sharing of memories was not only intensely emotional and incredibly healing, it was the time and the place to remember a war dog that was a big part of his life and who saved that life a thousand times over.

Spring 1966. A handsome, self-assured young man strode through the gates of the Infantry Training Centre in Ingleburn, New South Wales. Tall, sinewy and tanned with severely cropped fair hair and a natural military bearing, this 18-year-old looked every inch a soldier, proud in his khaki and ready for the world to take him on. Peter Haran had completed his six months of Army training and was looking to take his career into a specialist area. Through a corner of the perimeter fence it was possible to catch a glimpse of the Tracking Wing – the specialist school for training dogs and handlers for the task of detecting and seeking out the enemy in combat. A good Tracker dog hears and smells the enemy before they can be seen, detects landmines and tripwires ahead of any man, and gives chase at a speed to strike fear into the pursued.

Peter had often watched the dogs being put through their paces and had decided to enrol as a handler as soon as he could. He had been a dog lover since childhood and, thanks to his father, dogs played an important role in Haran family life, even before they moved to Australia from Zimbabwe. So it wasn't any wonder that the opportunity to combine his military career and his love of dogs was too good for Peter to resist. On the day of his interview with the second-in-command of the Tracking Wing, Warrant Officer Carter, Peter wanted to give it his best shot. This was his big chance to gain a place on the dog handler's training programme and what started as a short chat with Carter ended with Peter being told to report for duty the following day.

Delighted with his success, Peter turned to leave, only to feel that he was being watched. Just a few feet away in the shade of a tree sat a black Labrador cross. Fresh from his training session the dog sat gently panting, his glossy coat shining in the afternoon sun. Staring straight ahead, the dog had the young soldier firmly in his gaze. Peter stared back, all the time thinking how proud he would be to have a dog like that in his charge. Suddenly the dog stood up and moved to his handler's heel. As they walked together towards the kennel block the dog looked back at Peter, who noticed the animal's intense, velvety brown eyes. It was a look that Peter was to translate as 'I'll be seeing you later.'

It seemed that the long-legged black Labrador knew something that Peter didn't. In the meantime there was plenty of work to do. Peter and the eight other trainees had three weeks to convince Carter and his superior, Lieutenant French, that they were up to the job. The first week was spent away from the dogs, confined to a classroom learning about the capabilities of the dogs, the responsibilities of the visual Tracker (six of the nine men on the course were visual Trackers) and the neces-sary skills of the dog handler. Peter just wanted to be matched with a dog to get down to the work. From what he had observed looking through the fence, the training was conducted mostly outdoors with man and dog working together, getting to know each other and working as a coherent team. It was not sitting behind a desk. It was only later, when Peter was doing the job in Vietnam, that the advice of the trainer was to echo in his head many, many times over. He was told: obedience is a life-saver.

To be a member of the Combat Tracking Team was, he discovered, not just learning how to handle a dog physically; it was also to do with interpreting the dog's reactions, the terrain they were working in and reading the signs correctly. It was about living life on the end of a 20-foot leash, following an intelligent dog, running where he runs for as long as it takes to capture or corner the enemy. Lives depended on the Tracker dog's actions and the handler's interpretation. It's the partnership that holds the key to life or death, and the level of trust. Knowing that a dog will lock on to one scent and will follow that scent means trusting the dog to do exactly that. If the dog 'points' to indicate the enemy's presence then it's not to be ignored. If a dog can follow a simple instruction to 'sit' and 'stay' when its life and everyone else's around depends on it, then it's a partnership.

If you want to be a Tracker then being the one who is tracked is a good way of learning the dog's skills. 'For the next two days you're the enemy,' said Carter. 'Get the Viet Cong gear from the store hut.' Still without a dog at his side Peter and his training buddy, Blue Murray, were issued with rifles, blank ammunition, a backpack, a day's rations, a map and compass before being transported by Land Rover to Bulli Pass, the forested area near the Pacific Highway, south of Sydney. After replacing their usual uniforms with dirty civilian clothing to create a scent that could be tracked, the men set off with the challenge to reach their assigned destination ahead of the Tracker dog and his handler. A visual Tracker was also assigned to the dog's team. His job was to look for the physical signs that Peter and Blue would unknowingly leave in their wake (disturbed earth, footprints, clues in the flora and fauna) as they trudged in their sweat-sodden clothes to the finish point. The heat of the day was only part of the challenge. The convoluted route that was created to take the two trainee Trackers to the limit took them into creeks and through swathes of long grass and up muddy banks. There was no time to stop to notice bruises or scars or to rest.

Having run for the best part of the morning, the men were feeling exhausted. There was no sign of the Tracker dog, in fact there was no sign of anyone at all en route, and Peter took this to mean that they had outwitted their pursuers. They were almost at the checkpoint. The map showed another ditch and an incline, which had to mean more mud, but then it would be over and the men could celebrate the end of their ordeal and their apparent victory over the dog. But before they had time to celebrate the visual Tracker appeared out of nowhere to announce they had been under surveillance for some time. The dog had tracked them and 'pointed' to indicate their presence from across the clearing. The men were totally oblivious. 'Come, Caesar,' said the handler, offering his dog a welcome drink of water. The exercise was over and Caesar could stand down, which meant his handler could remove the dog's canvas working harness. Peter took a closer look at the dog that had made them look so foolish: it was the same black Labrador that had given him that knowing look on the day of his interview. So, his name was Caesar. He looked at the dog, exhausted and now snoring, his head settled on his handler's leg. At that moment, when the dog was only to be admired from afar, Peter remembered looking at the dog, saying to himself, 'Just how bloody good are you?'

More than anything Peter wanted a dog to work with. And a few days later, that's exactly what he got. The dog was not in the same class as Caesar, not even to look at. The only resemblance was that they were both more Labrador than anything else. This dog, introduced to Peter as Damien, was not only unusual to look at; he was difficult from the start. The dog simply wouldn't work for him and, as it turned out, he wouldn't work for anyone. Every opportunity this dog had to get into a fight with another dog he took it. Two minutes into the first training session Damien pulled to reach another dog and sent Peter flying backwards onto the ground. On day two of the partnership he went AWOL to find other dogs to fight with. At first Peter thought Damien was just a dog who needed to feel secure.

Certainly the close working relationship a Tracker dog had with his handler would convince any dog that he was needed, and the very physical nature of the work would ensure an outlet for Damien's excess energy. Peter wanted to remain positive and give Damien a chance but it was difficult when the dog took every opportunity to start a fight.

It was the day the dogs and their handlers were jammed into an old Studebaker bound for Bulli Pass that Damien convinced everyone that not all dogs can be trained to do something. The trainer thought the change of scenery could help the dog. Peter was less convinced but he was ever hopeful of an improvement. Careful to be last into the vehicle so he could sit close to the tailgate and execute a quick exit if he needed to, Peter put Damien under the seat so he could not make eye contact with any of the other dogs. They were happily dozing at their masters' feet, until the sound of the truck's wheels spinning in mud awoke everyone. The handlers pulled their dogs closer to their legs to keep them close and calm. But Damien had other ideas. Without Peter noticing, the dog had crawled under the bench and was within reach of the others. As the Studebaker struggled to get a grip on the land Damien chose his moment to launch an attack on his 11 colleagues.

The sound of high-pitched yelps of pain suddenly filled the back of the truck. Damien had one of the captive canines by the throat and still had his teeth in the other dog's flesh when Peter hurled him out of the truck. As the tarpaulin was removed from the back of the lorry, the rest of the dogs and handlers tumbled out at all angles, desperate to escape Damien's fangs. Everyone looked at Peter. What was he going to do with that dog of his?

The decision was taken out of Peter's hands. The next morning the trainer took a pistol from the armoury and headed for the kennel. His final comment to Peter: 'There are some dogs you can't train anytime.'

Peter had suffered for his dog's misdemeanours but after the incident in the truck, everyone could see that Damien would never have been Tracker material. His need to fight to the point of bloodshed proved that he was no one's ideal family pet either. He was beyond help.

So Peter was without a dog.

Australia's involvement in the Vietnam War had started in 1962. At first the commitment was a team of thirty advisers. By 1965 the commitment had risen to a battalion of the Australian Army. By 1966 a task force was provided involving all three branches of the Armed Forces but it was the Army that played the largest part. The US was already using dogs in Vietnam when the Australians sent out their first dog tracking teams in 1967. The Australian Combat Tracker dog training unit was specially created to train the dogs as trackers with the infantry. The very nature of the conflict had influenced the way the dogs were being prepared as this was jungle warfare with guerrilla tactics and the nearest parallel was the British-trained Tracker dogs used during the Malaya Campaign in the 1950s. The first of the Australian dogs to be trained this way graduated from the training school in Sydney in 1966. To be a part of one of the first teams to be used in Vietnam, Peter Haran needed a dog.

A few days later the news quickly spread through the unit that Caesar's handler had been reassigned to other duties, leaving the dog in need of a partner. Caesar needed a new handler and Peter needed a dog. He could hardly believe his luck. After the fiasco with Damien he now had the chance to display his new skills, and more than that, he was going to have what he considered the best dog around as his partner. Caesar, the dog who had caught his eye on his first day in the Tracking Wing, who had successfully tracked him down on a training exercise in Bulli Pass, was now in his charge.

Caesar had not been bred by the Army. He was one of thousands of dogs who entered the Services via the local stray dog's home. If the military scouts had not arrived when they did, this dog would have been destroyed and not had the chance to serve his country. His obvious trademark was his odd ears: the right one always erect and the left one bent due to a missing piece, but that never detracted from this dog's proud bearing. A handsome black Labrador with long legs and narrow shoulders, Caesar was an athletic mix of the classic Labrador and the Australian kelpie and had intelligence written all over his face. His eyes were always bright and alert but he had an attractive calmness that, in any other situation, would make anyone think that he was nothing more or less than an Aussie rural working dog. And he had one more quality that made him the perfect Tracker – he never gave up.

As luck or fate would have it, the Labrador's alert expression and lively disposition attracted the scouts to his kennel and within no time at all the three dollars had been paid over and the dog that was to be named Caesar was in the back of a Land Rover and on his way to the Infantry Training Centre. For an active dog that craved attention and a outlet for his exuberance, the training was ideal. The weeks in the stray dog's home had not dampened his spirit or his enthusiasm, which he now poured into his training. Passing every section with flying colours, Caesar became the blue-eyed boy at the Training Centre and an obvious candidate for being assigned to duties in Vietnam.

But there was work to do as a partnership before a posting was possible. First Peter and Caesar had to get to know each other and that was to begin with inheriting the dog and his 'uniform'. A Tracker dog required very little equipment but it all had to be accounted for in his handler's kitbag. The dog would wear, at all times, his collar with a disk bearing his Service number – for Caesar, D6NO3. Other necessities included the 20-foot-long dog leash that would keep the two paired throughout their 12 months' service in Vietnam, a canvas 'jacket' the dog would wear on manoeuvres plus his food, bowl, drinking water and towel. The dog travelled light, the handler did not!

Caesar was now officially Peter's responsibility and the man had only one fear – that he was not good enough for this incredible dog. But he need not have worried; the dog appeared to have enough confidence for both of them.

When news of the posting to Vietnam came through, Peter and his friend Denis Ferguson (forever after known as 'Fergie') were on the list to go. Caesar and Fergie's dog, Marcus, continued their training and grooming to attain perfect physical fitness in readiness for their flight and the job in hand. The dogs were going to experience extreme heat, long hours in harness and living between kennels, jungle and helicopters. What lay ahead was like nothing they had ever known before. The truth was, no one could prepare man or dog for what lay ahead. The conflict in Vietnam was like shifting sand and for some of the American and Australian soldiers out there already it was not immediately obvious how the dogs were going to help the situation.

By March 1967 Peter and Fergie knew they were going to be joining the 2nd Battalion, the Royal Australian Regiment (2 RAR) and, alongside Caesar and Marcus, they were transported by Land Rover to Richmond Air Base then by plane to Brisbane. From there it was a matter of settling in Enoggera, the Regiment's home, where 1,000 men were nearing the end of the intensive training that would see them through a year's fighting in Vietnam. The two men attended a final briefing and completed their pre-embarkation checks before they prepared their dogs for the flight out to Saigon. A giant C-130 Hercules transport plane awaited them.

On 7 May Caesar and Marcus boarded the Hercules. Strapped into the vast belly of the plane, the specially constructed dog crates were made secure for the journey. All around them sat the piles and piles of supplies also making the journey to Saigon that day. It seemed odd and wrong that the dogs should travel with the military hardware, but back in 1967 there was no specific category for listing war dogs. They came under 'engineers' stores', the same as barbed wire, shovels, explosives and ammunition. But the dogs were not alone. Peter and Fergie shared the same cold and draughty space and were close enough to the dogs to see their yellow eyes piercing the darkness. And they remained in view until the men took their first steps on Vietnamese soil.

Caesar and Marcus were now part of the first Australian Tracker teams in Vietnam. Each battalion would have two dogs and handlers, a cover man and, ideally, visual Trackers to pick up the physical clues such as turned leaves, scuffed trees and blood trails. The reality was that sometimes there were two dog and handler teams and other times just the dog and handler, no other support. The teams would be called in where there had been an engagement with the enemy and follow-up was required. The dog would then go in front of the patrol, following the enemy track. Man and dog would work together in the field, sleep, eat and live under the same roof or length of plastic sheeting. They would look out for each other as they rested and relieved themselves in the jungle. It was a 24/7 partnership and a friendship often put to the test.

The airbase in Saigon was jumping with activity. Stifling heat and the hot stench of aviation fuel hit the men square between the eyes. The air was thick with fumes and the noise of planes and helicopters landing or taking off every 45 seconds. It was not a dog-friendly environment but the men knew that dogs would have only one priority when they left their crates. There was never a dog 'toilet' but this time there was no dog space either, as every patch of land was devoted to storing, loading or servicing some kind of vehicle or weapon. Inside the base's perimeter fence the machinery of war was being tested and transported and made ready for the war. Outside it appeared that life for the local people carried on as normal. They went about their usual business but now under the watchful eye of the

American and Australian military. As Peter watched the world go by on the other side of the fence, Caesar had cocked his leg in full view of an old lady sitting in the street. She watched without showing a glimmer of emotion. Her stare disappeared right through them.

There wasn't time to take in the scenery. For now it was a hot, smelly and inhospitable place and those who noticed the dogs seemed confused by their presence. Peter recalled being approached by two US soldiers who seemed unimpressed with the idea of dogs 'chasing Charlie' (Charlie being the Viet Cong, Victor Charlie in the phonetic alphabet). One soldier hoped the dogs would 'bite Charlie's ass'. The other said the dogs had better get Charlie before 'Charlie eats the dogs'. Peter could not help feeling that the dog teams were regarded by many as being pointless. Were things really that bad that a Tracker team could be the butt of the joke? Volunteering for the Army was all that Peter wanted to do, but he knew enough from the news reports on the television and in the newspapers that men were being killed in Vietnam. He knew that every step he took in the jungle was to determine his survival.

However, it was not something he could afford to think about. There was a job to do.

A Caribou aircraft took the two men and their dogs on the final leg of their journey, to Luscombe Field in Nui Dat, the home of the Australian Task Force. Caesar and his friends were now a part of the war in Vietnam. There was no turning back.

Arriving at the base the first thing that hit the senses was the reeking stink of mildew, rotting sandbags and putrid vegetation that dominated the atmosphere. There was no escaping the red mud that appeared during each monsoon and coated everyone and everything, including the tents they slept in. Although exhausted from their flight in, the men felt compelled to make their basic living quarters a little more bearable and a little less soggy. It was never going to look like home but two days of tidying, re-arranging and making the best of what they had paid off. The cramped accommodation was dominated by the two cots where the men crashed out. The 'bathroom' consisted of an improvised 'basin' and a mirror that Peter took from a special leather shaving set that his parents had given him. He knew it would come into use one day and there it was nailed to a tree outside the tent.

As for the dogs, the Royal Engineers had constructed a set of very solidly built kennels. Again it was a building lacking in home comforts but the dogs seemed excited about it and it was one more thing packed with new smells and an area they could make their own. Besides, there was always their handlers' cots to lie on if given half the chance. Caesar did not complain about his new quarters, and Peter was around to supervise the play sessions that took place in and around the rubber trees, the long grass and piles of banana leaves.

As part of the 2nd Battalion's advance party to Vietnam, Caesar and Marcus had arrived two weeks ahead of everyone else. The others were travelling the slower route, by sea, on HMAS *Sydney*. It was a good opportunity for the Trackers to acclimatize as they would be working long hours in very hot conditions and they were not used to the humidity or the jungle terrain. On 30 May the slicks of Chinook helicopters started to bring in the rest of 2 RAR from the troopship at Vung Tau and, at the same time, ferried out the 6th Battalion who had completed their tour of duty. The Tracking Team was established in its six tents as part of the support company providing a service to the infantry, both Australian and American. Everyone was in place and the dogs were settled but it seemed the only thing that was happening was the rain.

Caesar was not a dog who liked rain but there was little chance to escape it, especially for anyone on guard duty. Not long after arriving at the base, and while on operations in the jungle, Peter and Caesar were assigned guard duty and quickly took up position, Peter rigging up a small shelter against the elements. The shelter was just a length of plastic sheeting the men called a hootchie. Snug beneath the shelter Peter was finding the guard duty bearable – the problem was, Caesar was not and he had his eyes on the hootchie. There had to be room under there for one long-legged soggy Labrador surely? Well, Caesar thought so and decided to manoeuvre himself under the sheeting a bit of his body at a time: first his head, then his chunky shoulders, followed by the rest of him, right down to the dripping tail.

It wasn't easy for a long-legged Labrador to slip into a space unnoticed and no matter how much he tried to make himself more compact, Caesar failed miserably. Sitting with the dog's legs somehow sloped over his stomach and having to put up with the constant nudging for space, not to mention the smell of warm wet dog right under his nose, Peter eventually lost his temper and pushed Caesar out into the rain. But Caesar wasn't having any of it and turned tail to come back under the hootchie. Unable to take so much dog in one small space Peter, in one crazy moment, stood up, trod on his rifle, tripped on his webbing and brought the hootchie down on Caesar, who took off into the pouring rain with the plastic sheet trailing after him. It was a learning experience for both man and dog and one never to repeat.

As embarrassing experiences go Peter was to suffer one of the worst of all in Vietnam. Everything came into the camp by helicopter and went out the same way. Helicopters were a fact of life, ever present and unavoidable, but Caesar went crazy around them.

Caesar and helicopters didn't mix and as always with this dog, Peter had to learn the hard way.

Being assigned to Ready Reaction status meant being ready to move out on a helicopter to any location where they were needed. In 10 minutes there had to be a bag ready to leave containing human and dog food and water for both man and dog. Peter had 'greened' his rifle stock to remove the shine and strapped a shell dressing to his rifle with black tape so it could be used to plug a wound in an emergency. He was ready when the call came down the line: 'Trackers out!'

Caesar heard the slow and mesmerizing thud of the Huey helicopter rotor blades before Peter. Weaving, jumping and frothing at the mouth, Caesar was making Peter nervous. Was this the way the dog was going to behave every time a helicopter was in sight? If so, poor Caesar would be a constant embarrassment. But to Peter's relief the dog settled down in a small space in the body of the helicopter which, after that day, he ran to each time.

Climbing up and over Nui Dat hill the yellow, brown colours of the rubber trees gave way to the mottled greens of the lush jungle vegetation. Bamboo, paddy fields and the dense forest, or 'J' as the Australian diggers called it, crept into view. They were nearing the spot where factions of the Viet Cong were known to be hiding out. No one knew if this meant sections of the professionals from the National Liberation Front with AK-47s and RPGs, or a guerrilla group with a machine gun, or peasants wielding rifles. The identity and strength of the enemy could be that diverse.

The helicopter landed and Peter quickly harnessed Caesar for action. This was it. Their first Track and Peter hardly needed to utter the words 'Seek 'em out!' as the dog was ready to go. There was no need to look for any more of a visible clue than the trail of blood on the path ahead. It was all happening very fast and Peter felt the pressure of the first-time search, and the more urgent pressure to not 'mess up'. In this situation, messing up cost lives. But Caesar was moving purposefully ahead, his nose seemingly stuck to the ground. He was following the blood trail with the cover man and company commander in support with SLR (self-loading rifle) and M60 in hand. All attention was on Caesar.

They needed that point. They knew the enemy was there and then … suddenly Peter disappeared. He had fallen into an enemy weapon pit. He crawled out and saw Caesar standing stock still on the track ahead. Recognizing the sign, Peter shortened the leash and said, 'Get 'em boy!' Within 50 yards, the dog pointed, drawing attention to a white shrouded body on the ground. Peter recalled that the body moved, but not with signs of life. It was covered in white butterflies that rose into the air like spirits. That was the first time Peter had seen a dead Viet Cong. The Trackers had led their party to the site of a labyrinth of bunkers, which needed searching urgently before the enemy returned.

When searching the surrounding villages everywhere took on the look and feel of a place with a secret. Every face, young and old, could be a Charlie. No one could be exempt from suspicion. When Caesar and the rest of the team were deployed with 2 RAR's tour of Lang Phuoc Hai in the south of the country and the area known as Long Green (due to its shape and colour on a map), the battalion was under orders to conduct sensitive searches of the houses and outhouses with minimal distress to the villagers. The terrain lent itself perfectly to enemy activity with hides and bunkers and tunnels known to be hidden over a vast area.

Caesar and Peter remained on duty as the searches were carried out. Unlike his handler, Caesar was uninterested in observing the local people, their customs and costumes. For Caesar the most exciting part of each operation was – everything. He loved being released from his kennel and then jumping into the Land Rover and arriving at the helipad where he could bark and froth at the mouth just at the thought of getting on board the Huey. It all happened so quickly. Soon the team was airborne and heading south-west over the rubber plants, with only their imagination to tell them what could lie ahead.

Caesar did not sleep until the search had been completed. Explosions could be heard throughout the night but the dog did not rest until the helicopter returned in the morning to take the Tracker team back to Nui Dat. This had been a test for man and dog and both had done their duty and survived. Survival was the best you could hope for when you faced an enemy that had the identity of a chameleon and a terrain to match.

Dog-loving Peter was interested in the welfare of the animals too and in one village he was intrigued by a stray dog that seemed to be generally ignored despite his friendly nature. The dog seemed used to human contact and that was good to see in an environment so full of mistrust and unease. But clearly there was a reason why his attempts at affection were repeatedly rebuffed by the villagers. Peter couldn't bear to see the dog's sadness and despite all the warnings about disease, including rabies, decided to extend a hand of friendship to this lonely dog.

'C'mon fella,' urged Peter. 'I won't hurt you.' Crouching down to talk to the dog, Peter offered him a piece of biscuit just to show he meant no harm. The dog, a thin and wasted German shepherd, was wary of the food. But Peter understood. He was prepared to spend a little time to get the dog's trust. Talking in a soft, low voice Peter noticed the dog's eyes soften and his ears prick up as if to say 'thank you for your company'. Then, as the dog stood to move a little closer, Peter could see that he had a head injury. He had blood in his fur and a lump the size of an egg on his head and as Peter moved closer there was something else: the dog had half his skull missing – the sloppy grey mass on his head was his exposed brain. A piece of his skull had been blown clean away, and it would obviously be just a matter of time before this dog joined the other casualties of the war. Peter looked at the dog. He had not been able to see the dog's injuries from where he was sitting but even then he was still a stray dog looking for affection, just as Caesar had been. But this dog had been so badly affected by the war that he was just one more of the walking dead. Peter reached for Caesar and hugged him. 'I promise to look after you,' he said. 'You will not suffer like that.'

When a dog saves your life it's not something you forget. If a dog saves your life six times, he's a hero and that's what Caesar came to be for Peter Haran, especially on the day the men stopped for lunch in a paddy field. Taking a break from a village search Peter and 10 other diggers took the advice of their platoon commander and moved off the road and into the nearby paddy field. The men settled in to eat from cans, boil water for drinks and enjoy a smoke when they noticed what looked like an argument breaking out between their commander and a local soldier. No one could hear what was being said but both men were wearing aggressive expressions and gesticulating towards the field. Suddenly the soldier stepped forward, cupped his hands to his mouth and yelled: 'Everyone stay where you are. Do not move. You're having lunch in a minefield.'

Peter felt the colour drain from his face. The guy must be joking. Right? No, he wasn't joking. And there was another question: can a dog set off a mine? Peter turned towards Caesar who had wandered off to relieve himself. He was about to leave his spot 20 metres away when Peter held up his hand, palm facing the dog. 'Caesar!' The dog looked at him. 'Caesar, stay. Caesar, sit.' He obeyed and looked directly into Peter's eyes as if to say, 'What's next?' 'Caesar, down!' The dog slipped down onto his stomach. 'Good dog Caesar. Stay.' The dog followed every instruction perfectly, his eyes locked onto Peter's and his big pink tongue lolling out of his mouth.

Now Peter had to clear a path to get him out. If the dog veered from the path and tripped a mine, the men would have been killed outright. Using their knives the men prodded the ground. Peter cleared a circle around himself and then gently worked out towards Caesar who lay motionless, his black coat glistening and heaving in the sun. If Caesar had moved from his mark many lives would have been lost. Moments later the deep thud of a Huey brought some reassurance but it was short-lived for Peter. He prayed Caesar wouldn't dash for the helicopter rotor blades, the way he usually did. One false move now and all hell would break loose. But Caesar didn't run and bite at the rotor blades. Not this time. The dog, like the men, was exhausted. They had stopped for lunch in a paddy field and then remained in the heat of the afternoon working through a minefield, in danger not just from the mines but also from heatstroke. The hours of concentration had affected Caesar and he didn't have the strength to confront a helicopter. The helicopter was not his enemy today – it carried an engineer mine-detecting team. Fear still showed on the faces of the men and the dog after they had extricated themselves. They had cheated death that afternoon. With sweat pouring down his face in torrents, Peter had managed to keep his cool and maintain the all-important eye contact with Caesar. 'Is that your dog up front?' asked one of the others. 'Thank Christ he does what he's told!'

It had been an eventful day, to say the least, and for Peter a day of contemplation. The constant risk of death – from both the enemy and the environment – made each 24 hours that passed an exercise in survival. As Peter headed to the kennels with Caesar to bed him down for the night his friend Fergie waved him over. He had some bad news. While Caesar and his colleagues had been escaping from the mine-infested paddy field, his fellow Tracker dog Cassius had fought and lost a battle against heatstroke. His handler Norman Cameron was in pieces. This dog had been on an exercise in the dunes at Vung Tau with 7 RAR Tracking Team when he collapsed with heat exhaustion. Norman saw the dog's eyes roll in their sockets and then he was foaming at the mouth.

It was not the first time this had happened but this time there was no transport available to take man and dog to the American hospital unit. After draping the dog in wet towels there was only one thing to do: Norman lifted Cassius like a baby in his arms and ran for the hospital over three miles away. The dog was suffering badly. He was hyperventilating and clearly in a state of distress despite Norman's attempts to revive him with water from the drinking bottles. Norman was just a few hundred yards away from help when they walked into an ambush. There was a brief gunfight, which left four Viet Cong dead on the road. Cass was now in a critical state. Four hours had passed since he collapsed. Norman tried his best to cool the dog but he now had to follow orders and stay and wait for transport. When it finally came, it had been five hours since the dog collapsed and Cassius lived just another 30 minutes when they finally got him to the hospital. A post mortem revealed that most of the dog's internal organs had literally cooked in the heat. It was a shocking way for this war dog to end his days. Cassius had been the first of the Australian Trackers and paved the way for those, like Caesar, who were to follow. It was a terrible way for him to go.

Peter was about to relax for the evening but the call came again to 'Scramble' and so it was back into clean jungle greens. By now the drill was finely tuned: dog and handler with backpack carrying rations, fresh water and a basic medical kit, the dog's leash, rifle and ammunition. The battle dress in this terrain was greens and a floppy hat; road convoys required a flak jacket and a helmet. Helmets were never worn in the jungle.

As Peter harnessed-up Caesar in his canvas jacket the forward scout explained why they had been called upon. He showed them an area littered with spent cartridges alongside a track that wove around some bamboo. The Viet Cong had taken a taste of the mighty M60 tank, thanks to the forward section gunner but, like phantoms in the night, they had disappeared into the dense undergrowth. Only the cartridges and a pool of blood remained. It was now Caesar's job to track the VC for the rifle platoon. As always, Caesar was ready to start the search. Peter had held back, waiting for a formal order to 'Seek 'em out!' It seemed strange to him to just start a search in that way, but word was the search had to start immediately.

Armoured personnel carriers surrounded the area. The Viet Cong might have regarded the Long Green area as theirs but there was no way the Australians were going to let them just walk in and take it over. Caesar stopped for his customary 'relief' and followed Peter's orders to 'Seek 'em. Get 'em!' There was blood all along the path and indications that the well-trodden track had seen its fair share of military boots or heavy footwear. There was little sign of the villagers' soft shoes here. Caesar was following a strong scent and it was all the scout and the cover man could do to keep up with the Labrador as he worked on about 50 yards ahead of Peter.

As the bush thickened, Caesar glued his nose nearer to the track. Peter determined that the platoon had searched either side of the track but not the middle section that had brought them to a T-junction on the road. Caesar stopped dead. It was an open area with only silence surrounding them and it was the silence that suddenly spooked Peter. 'Don't stop. What's the matter with you Caesar? Keep searching,' Peter hissed as he urged Caesar on, afraid the dog had missed something in the middle section of the road. Then he remembered his classroom training: if the dog acts in an uncharacteristic way, stop and ask why that could be. With his head to the ground, Caesar turned and walked towards his handler and then promptly sat on his foot. Then he pushed on Peter's legs. It was then Peter realized the new insistent behaviour was Caesar's way of saying, 'There's something wrong here.' There *was* something wrong. A few seconds later a bright orange-and-white flash detonated across the ground.

They had walked into a Viet Cong minefield. Thrown face down, Peter lay on the ground. Suddenly the air was filled with cries of 'I'm hit. I'm hit!' 'Mines! Don't move!' Casualties lay all around. Some lay motionless and others crawled to help their comrades on the ground. The platoon commander had been badly wounded, as had the signaller. Charlie had laid mines on both sides of the track and had run a line down the middle. It was a trick and everyone fell for it. Peter felt responsible for the misery. Hurt and depressed, he thought over his actions and wondered how he could have overlooked a basic Tracker rule –

trust your dog. He needed water and provisions for Caesar. The atmosphere was quiet for a while but there was no hostility between the men. It was Caesar who gave Peter the look, the 'Why on earth did you do that? You should have trusted me.'

The Viet Cong had planted a cocktail of explosive devices along the track and at specific points, all of which was designed to cause maximum damage. What Caesar had indicated included two M16 'jumping jacks' on the main track that were wired with detonator cord to an unexploded bomb. The engineers thought the bomb could be a naval shell or a 500lb from an air strike. It would have taken the whole platoon, even the company out. The scout reached down to Caesar's nose: 'Thank sweet Jesus for you,' he said, stroking the dog's head.

Peter sat for a good while on his own thinking of the 'what ifs?': what if he had pushed Caesar on, trodden on the M16 mine and detonated the big charge? He would have died at 19 years of age and the blast would have sent shards of burning shrapnel into everyone around him and created a massive crater on Long

Green. Caesar could have been lost too. But he was not lost, and the blast would have done more damage if Caesar had not pointed when he did. It could clearly have been worse. As one of the others said to Peter Haran, 'The dog's your salvation, mate.'

A dog in a war zone can be the most tangible and comforting reminder of home, a symbol of normality when life is anything but normal. The Trackers were working dogs, war dogs trained for a specific duty in a particular location, and more than that, they protected their handlers in vulnerable situations. They shared their food, accommodation, space and company almost every hour of the day and night. It was a close working relationship that created a bond based on trust and mutual respect, but outside 'work' hours the dogs wanted to do what every dog wants to do – play!

When Peter and Fergie set eyes on a 44-gallon oil drum they didn't see scrap metal, they saw the perfect dog bath. It didn't take long for the bath to become a daily feature of Tracker dog life. It was the perfect way to play at the end of a very exhausting day. The men always made time to play with the dogs before they went into their kennels and especially when they returned from an operation and needed to release some of the tension and stress. Caesar and Marcus were good friends so they would play together like puppies and the men loved to see the dogs rolling in the grass and bounding around like any pet dogs you might see anywhere in the world. The dogs just happened to be Labradors playing in the world's most volatile playground in 1968.

The Vietnam jungle kept many deadly secrets, not just its array of poisonous snakes and insects but the contents of the thousands of bunkers and the labyrinth of tunnels that threaded through the villages and the countryside. They were there, even if the Australian and American Forces could not always find them. Just like the M16 'jumping jack' mine, the grenade and the expertly wielded machete: they were there, waiting, even if you couldn't see them. The stealthy and deadly nature of guerrilla warfare tested every soldier's courage, character and determination to stay alive and his desire to win. It broke the spirit of some and took the life of many – and so with the dogs.

The United States Army had 2,000 dogs assigned to duties in Vietnam. They provided support as guard and patrol dogs, as well as explosive search dogs and mine detectors. The Australian Task Force boasted 11 dogs, all black Labradors, trained specifically to track the position of the Viet Cong forces and their weapons, explosives and ammunition. To the call 'Task Force out' the dogs would take up position with their handlers come rain, shine or monsoon. Although a small force, they were very effective and much sought after even by the Americans. As Peter and Caesar were on Ready status, anything could happen. On several occasions they assisted the US Cavalry when they called for a Tracker dog and the Americans soon got used to Caesar and his unusual helicopter fetish. By the time the chopper sent to collect man and dog arrived Caesar invariably had been waiting about 30 minutes and the deep drone of its arrival made him so excited that he threw himself into the open doorway, dragging Peter, at speed, behind him. Peter hated the embarrassment but always covered for the dog: 'He just loves helicopters!' The Huey was the one Caesar saw most and the one he was always trying to launch himself into.

Until January 1968 the Australian forces had confined their activity to Phuoc Tuy province, but then the American command ordered a move to the bases of Long Khanh and Bien Hoa provinces on the border with the North. Two thousand men moved north. Peter and Caesar joined Fergie and Marcus and the rest of the Task Force and jumped in trucks bound for Route 15. The dogs loved a ride in the open cabin. Caesar's long legs meant he could happily rest his on the dashboard, but shorter Marcus had to be content with a front seat.

Open sandbags, overflowing latrines, collapsing bunkers and weapon pits made the place look such a shambles all round that the men decided to get together for a big tidy-up. It would be hard work but rewarding. However, by 1 February there was no time for the great tidy-up. The Tet Offensive was underway and the Viet Cong was targeting every major base in the south. The roads and sky filled with every kind of military vehicle and aircraft. The helicopters ran day and night. The attack was vicious and the country was ablaze.

The men dug in. Peter, along with Caesar and several other men, were in a fighting bunker. Peter had stretched his flak jacket on the ground for his dog's comfort. It was going to be a long night. An explosion rocked the base. Caesar gave out a yelp as if he was being strangled so Peter put his arms around his dog. Caesar was in the grip of a shaking fit. They were being mortared, and the country all around appeared to be on fire. Caesar was terrified and now it was Peter's turn to comfort his dog – repayment for all those other times when Peter looked to Caesar for his unconditional affection. 'There was a time back then when I found myself praying. I hadn't prayed since I was a child, asking Jesus to keep me safe but I looked down to my filthy boots and the dog leash and I said – God bless my dog.'

Shortly after, the Trackers returned by road convoy to Nui Dat as 3 RAR moved in. It had been a savage exchange to witness and there had been fighting in the streets that had spilt over to exchanges in the houses too. The fear of more violence hung in the air. The return to Nui Dat was a good one even though bad news awaited them. Their Tracker friend Garry 'Polly' Polglase had been killed in a shooting accident. The Trackers had lost one dog, Cassius, and now a handler too. It was bad and demoralizing news. Julian would have to have a new handler, unless Garry's mother was successful in her request to have the dog returned to her.

Garry's death had set everyone thinking about their own mortality. The Tracker dogs endeared themselves to their handlers by being intelligent, loyal, and 'someone' to talk to who would never judge. The dogs became as essential to the soldiers as their 60lb kitbags and so it was no wonder that they all wanted to take their dogs back to Australia after the war.

With only two months' service left to do in Vietnam, Peter Haran was posted to Bear Cat, the home of the 9th Brigade. He had requested that his last few weeks be spent somewhere 'quiet': Bear Cat had a reputation for being a large military complex that was attacked quite frequently. After the horror of the Tet Offensive Peter had hoped that he and his colleagues could be spared more potential attacks by the Viet Cong. The site was grubby and shabby just like most of the bases Peter knew, but he felt particularly disillusioned and angry at this one. The Trackers had been told that they could not, under any circumstances, take the dogs back home to Australia with them. This was devastating news. While Fergie busied to get the dogs ready for the replacement handlers who would be arriving any day, Peter went for a walk. The pain, anguish and horror that he had lived through over the previous 10 months had started to play on the young soldier's mind. It was a good job that his 12-month draft was coming to an end. He needed it to end and so did Caesar. Peter had noticed that the physical changes he experienced the dog was showing too: both were leaner animals, exhausted, distracted, sometimes angry, sometimes introverted. They had been through 10 months of war together and they had the battle scars to prove it.

Peter had no idea why he and Fergie and the dogs were at Bear Cat or what they were going to be doing. Caesar was with him and together they reported for duty. The job that was waiting for him was helicopter air traffic control. Had they not noticed his dog? For

Peter this was a final bizarre twist in his career which only made him more resentful of the situation. The previous week he had been dealing with body bags and tracking the enemy in the jungle; now suddenly he was an air traffic controller.

After doing his stint in air traffic control Peter returned to the kennel for Caesar. He told him all about what had happened and gave the big dog a hug. A visit to the cook house resulted in a bone each for Caesar and Marcus so the day had not gone so badly after all. But there was one thing left to do. On his travels, Peter had noticed there was a swimming pool on site. Fergie was a little worried that the authorities might not like the dogs going in, but that didn't matter because they decided to swim at midnight. No one would see and no one would know. The dogs would love it!

The swimming pool was the answer to all their problems of the day and it was the first time the dogs had been able to swim in water like that in ages. But the midnight swim was about to be disturbed. An officer, hearing the splashing, had decided to investigate and discovered the two men and their dogs. The expression of fury on the man's face said it all. The 'pool' was in fact the camp's supply of drinking water.

The stay at Bear Cat was cut short and Peter and Fergie were posted to Battalion Headquarters. They were still working with the dogs until the official hand-over to the new handlers, but for now they would be on call, attending situations where a Tracker was needed perhaps by rifle companies. In the meantime they would be part of an operation to establish defensive perimeters in the bush. It meant taking Caesar on a short lead and walking through vines, bamboo and scrub, which is difficult with a dog. The dog lead was forever getting entangled. It was also very hot work and Caesar was not happy from the start. Peter had plenty of water for them both to drink but the dog was panting heavily and it seemed unfair to take him through this all over again. Then Caesar flopped onto his stomach. For one brief and horrid moment all Peter could think about was Norman Cameron and how he lost Cassius to heatstroke. This was not the way for Caesar to go. This was not right at all.

'I'm losing my dog,' shouted Peter. 'I'm losing my dog.' Untangling the leash Peter swept Caesar up into his arms. He knew he needed to reach the medical centre or the veterinary surgeon as soon as was humanly possible. Peter did not stop running until he reached the vet's office and demanded help for his dog. Caesar was examined and treated for the collapse. Although it was no longer in his control Peter decided that Caesar would not suffer like that again. The thought that his friend could die like that was too much to bear.

On his last morning Peter packed his steel trunk and loaded the rest of his possessions into a container that would go ahead to the troopship HMAS *Sydney*. Then he lay on his bed and read and polished his boots in an attempt to avoid the inevitable. There was one last duty to perform and Fergie had agreed that Peter would go to the kennel block first. 'Caesar saw me coming and jumped up while Marcus was in his favourite position, on his back with his legs in the air, snoring. I walked up to the fence and stuck my hand in to receive a playful bite.' With tears close to the surface, Peter spoke to Caesar:

'I gotta go, you gotta stay, that's the way they run this war. You've got a new boss, but I don't ever want you to forget me, I won't forget you …'

The two dogs watched Peter walk away and even though he heard Caesar pick up his bowl and then drop it, as he always did, Peter resisted the temptation to look back. Stifling the tears with his fist, Peter Haran walked away that first day of June 1968.

Eleven Tracker dogs left Australia for Vietnam – none returned. It was a bitter pill for the men to swallow. Denis Ferguson (Fergie) offered to pay the $2,000 costs for the administration and quarantine fees to enable him to bring Marcus home but his request was denied.

Rats –

Delta 777

'Rats was like an oasis of friendship
in a desert of sadness.'

(Sergeant Major Evans, Welsh Guards)

January 1979: a crisp winter morning and a four-man 'brick' patrol was on duty in the town of Crossmaglen, South Armagh. Plumes of cold breath rose into the cool air as the tread of heavy, black boots cracked the silence on the streets. Brick Commander, Sergeant Kevin Kinton of 2 Company, 1st Battalion Grenadier Guards, was leading the way. A small, scruffy, rust-brown dog jogged at his heels.

Experience had taught Kinton to be wary of parked cars and he ordered his men to take to the middle of the road, not the roadside, to avoid a purple car parked at the kerbside. Better to take the risk of being picked off by a sniper than accept the virtual certainty of being blown to pieces by a car bomb. They were coming to the end of their patrol and were now close to the heavily guarded gates to the British Army base when another patrol approached. They were, in Army terminology, 'working the pavements': two soldiers taking each side of the road. The little dog left Kinton's heels. Maybe he decided to say hello to the soldiers in the other brick. Maybe he saw a friend from the base or just preferred to go into town with the others rather than return to barracks with Kinton. Whatever his reason the bristly mongrel wagged his fox-like tail as if to say 'see you later chaps', and trotted away. As Kinton and his men entered the huge barbed-wire topped gates, their grey frosted morning flashed orange. Time stood still. One soldier took the full blast and ran, engulfed in flames. A cloud of black ash and burning debris fell as the others fought to smother the fire covering their friend's body. It was most likely a radio-controlled petrol bomb placed in the boot of the purple car. The IRA would sometimes mix explosives with petrol to create the effect of a firebomb. By adding a ball of soap-powder flakes the explosion would force a spray of flaming soap mixture into the air. It would stick to and scorch anything and anyone it touched.

Fire and ash filled the sky. The sound of soldiers shouting orders mingled with the rumble of an armoured car and the distant thud of a helicopter. Soldiers attended to their injured friend, his clothes blackened and smouldering. The purple car was a raging ball of flames covering a dark metal skeleton. As the cold air smothered the heat and the smoke began to clear, Kinton caught sight of another casualty. Singed and smelling of burnt fur, the little brown dog had limped his way back to the main gates of the camp. His coat spattered in the soapy mixture released in the explosion, the dog was badly burnt and half his tail was missing.

Once more the dog had endured the same horrors as his soldier friends. His desire to run with the men on duty had earned him their respect. Over and over he proved that he was not afraid. That day, the soldiers nearly lost a comrade and their faithful little mascot dog lost half his tail. But it was not the beginning or the end of this dog's relationship with the British soldiers. It was one more chapter in the story of a remarkable dog called Rats, Army number Delta 777, the 'soldier dog' of Northern Ireland.

Mystery surrounds the real date that Rats joined the British Army. The sectarian 'Troubles' (as history has labelled them) in Northern Ireland attracted the presence of the British Army from 1969 onwards. Regiments arrived and then left four or five months later, each soldier spending their tour of duty constantly on the front line defending the territory and protecting the people who came under Sovereign rule. For the soldiers who served in Northern Ireland it was, in their words, the worst kind of guerrilla warfare, fought against a politically feverish terrorist group, the IRA, fuelled by Protestant and Catholic differences. During the height of the unrest in the 1970s the province was a part of the United Kingdom where even hardened soldiers knew they were wise to feel fear when they walked the streets. It was not a safe place for a soldier or a dog.

Rats grew up in Crossmaglen. On the surface, this small Ulster town was nothing more than a collection of houses, a church, a primary and a secondary school and 13 public houses, serving a population of just over a thousand people. Lying on the River Fane, this seemingly tranquil place boasted a castle, a heritage of fine lace making and a typically large market square where local farmers brought produce and where the towns-folk met to trade and talk. The place was no stranger to the bustle and chatter of an active community but the memorials in the square were testament to a darker facet of this community's identity. A memorial 'to those who have suffered for Irish freedom' stood a stone's throw away from a statue erected in memory of a British paratrooper killed by an IRA bomb. Blood ran on the streets of Crossmaglen and bullet holes peppered its walls and walkways. Republican and Catholic, the town was a strange dichotomy: it was both peaceful Irish community and a war zone.

It was the location of Crossmaglen that controlled and maintained the air of simmering hostility and the reason why its inhabitants kept a self-protecting silence. Crossmaglen was a frontier town. It lay just one and a half miles from the border between Northern Ireland and the Republic of Ireland to the south, across which the terrorists slipped at will. No one knew if it was safe to speak to anyone, so they chose caution and said nothing at all. The natural warmth of the Irish had to be stalled as anyone showing any friendly behaviour towards the soldiers could risk reprisals.

Of course talking to a dog was quite different and it was here, in an environment of fear and hostility, that Rats came into contact with British soldiers for the first time. Like them he often patrolled the Ardross estate on the outskirts of Crossmaglen. It was his territory and where he ate and slept, although there was nothing visible to eat or to sleep on. The grim grey houses looked in on each other as if they were ganging up on anyone who dared step too close. Certainly the soldiers experienced a palpable sense of intimidation from each net-curtained window. There was rare comfort to be found there for a stray dog either, although Rats never gave up hope and never deviated from his daily routine: first an early morning tour of the houses, paying particular attention to the odd one or two where he had found or scrounged a scrap in the past.

Tour complete he headed for the wasteland that stretched like a no-man's land beyond the houses. Nothing more than a bare patch of earth this place had once known grass and maybe there had even been a playground for the children, but neglect and the persistent Irish rain had reduced it to part scrubland and quagmire. Tethered piebald horses left to fend for themselves dragged their dry lips over the ground in the hope that they could conjure up a blade of grass to eat. And stray dogs snapped at their hooves for sport. Rats set himself apart from the pack. He was always his own dog and that's one reason why he endeared himself to the soldiers.

He could have attached himself to any of the British soldiers that served in Crossmaglen, and maybe he did in part, but the history of this mascot dog started to be plotted in 1978 thanks to 42 Commando Royal Marines. The regiment, assigned its six-month tour of duty in Armagh, decided to tolerate the playful antics of this persistent little dog and it all began with boot-laces. Rats loved them and the men admired this play-ful rust-coloured puppy-like animal for stepping forward and fearlessly lunging at the soldiers' big black boots and making a grab for the long laces. The locals may have wondered why such a small dog didn't fear a kick from those boots but he didn't. It was fun and fun was a big part of Rats's personality. Anyone asked to give their first impressions of Rats would say 'scruffy'! Then dirty, flea-ridden, revolting, determined, cheeky, charming, happy, intelligent and loyal to his friends. He was all of that and so much more besides. Corgi-like in looks and stature, Rats stood about eighteen inches off the ground on four sturdy legs. His body was as bristly as a broom head and his fox-like face was topped off by a pair of fox-like ears. And where he wasn't coloured copper and brown on the top he was (after a bath) a dazzling white on his chest and underbelly. What 42 Commando saw when they first met Rats was the muddy, scruffy version, and not a puppy at all but a dog that had already seen six or seven years of life in the bomb-scarred border town. This dog had been born into the Troubles.

To find such a happy little dog in such a dismal place was a pleasant surprise to the soldiers, who had soon became accustomed to being largely ignored by the human residents of the town. The game of tugging boot-laces with this playful stray became a regular feature of the patrol of Ardross. After a short while the soldiers even looked for the cheeky brown mongrel. They told their comrades to look out for him too. They didn't need to feed him; he was happy to have their attention and he gave them a cheerful respite from their isolated duties. But it was Rats who decided that he was going to stay with his new friends and one day he simply followed them 'home'.

Home, to the outside world, did not have many fireside comforts. The high steel fences, rolls of barbed wire and concrete towers of the British Army base in County Armagh looked forbidding by day and night. The site took in the old police station, which was clad with sheets of corrugated iron and hidden behind thick walls of barbed wire to protect the helipad. Offices, accommodation and the cookhouse shared the confines of the narrow building which just about had room for a small brown dog. His first bed was a blanket on the floor of the briefing room. His second bed was any vacant or warm and occupied bunk he could squeeze into.

It didn't take long for Rats to settle in and soon he was a constant member of the Army's daily patrols. He had an unusual waddle rather than a walk but it didn't hamper his speed in following the soldiers. His loyalty to his soldier friends was instant and he was quick to learn that he could be useful to the troops. When he was out on manoeuvres Rats would sense the approach of strangers and warned the soldiers with a soft growl. His canine sense of hearing being so much more acute than a human's, the advance warning saved lives in an ambush situation. Soon Rats's reputation as a lucky mascot spread and he was in demand by almost all brick commanders. Some saw a dog as a liability rather than an asset to a patrol, but one good experience with the dog was enough to convince them of Rats's loyalty.

Regiments came and went in Crossmaglen. Faces changed with the arrival and departure of the ever-present helicopters that flew from dawn to dusk between six locations. Company commanders came over from the mainland four or five days ahead of their men. They had probably spent three or four months familiarizing themselves with the terrain and the problems they would face on arrival. Section commanders would be in position a week before the start of their tour and finally the men of the three platoons that would form each company on duty arrived on site. The airlifting and dropping of the men was well rehearsed for security and accuracy: the helicopter dropped eight men in and lifted eight men out and repeated this until the operation was complete. As the men of 42 Commando Royal Marines departed in October 1978 they handed over to 2 Company, 1st Battalion Grenadier Guards, and brick commander Sergeant Kevin Kinton was one of two non-commissioned officers (NCOs) in the advance party. He was heading in for his first tour of Northern Ireland.

Like most soldiers arriving for the first time, the view of Crossmaglen from the relative safety of the helicopter made him wonder how it could be the same place his colleagues had described as a 'hell on earth'. It looked so peaceful, not a soul on the streets and no sign of the dangers he had been preparing for. As his helicopter descended towards the helipad Kinton saw two Marines waiting to take their places on the ride out and two dogs waiting patiently in the shadow of the rotor blades. One was a large black Labrador, who was later introduced as Fleabus, and the other a small, scruffy brown mongrel with perky ears and what looked like a grin on his face. Neither dog moved as Kinton landed and ran from the helicopter.

Following his orders he dumped his kit on his bunk, collected boots, flak jacket and battle kit from stores and made ready for duty. He left the base through the huge metal gates and took his first ground-level look at Crossmaglen. It looked less like the cosy village he had seen from the air. But that first night seemed quiet on the streets as the soldiers set up vehicle checkpoints – always a necessary security measure while the Army was carrying out a transfer of kit and building supplies, known as an Op Tonnage, from Belfast. The town was closed down. It was the only way to ensure the safety of the Army vehicles on the road. That night, Kinton caught sight of the little brown dog he had seen earlier at the helipad. This time he was at the heels of a Marine. The sight of the man, never mind that he was in battle dress, with a dog at his side, seemed so normal. Kinton recalled: 'I thought, how could death and danger be equated with such a familiar sight?'

After two hours on duty Kinton could sleep for two before going back to his duties on the vehicle checkpoint. In the morning his company commander, Major Charles Woodrow QGM, requested Kinton report to the Marine brick commander he was to replace. The Marine knew there was only one way to explain the complexities and the dangers of patrolling the streets of Crossmaglen and that was to go out there. Two Marines and Grenadiers Sergeant Kinton and Sergeant Keith Regan, the medic, made up the brick that morning. And there was one addition: the brown dog who jogged jauntily at the commander's feet.

The Saracen armoured car, or Scarrycan, that Kinton had seen in position by a derelict house the night before had only just moved away as his patrol approached. It crossed his mind that the Opposition (Army speak for the IRA) had no time to enter the house after the Scarrycan left. It seemed more vital to move away from the telegraph pole on the opposite side of the road where fresh earth lay at the base. It was a gamble. Always a gamble. A bomb could be hidden by the house, or a mine could be placed at the base of the pole or both could be safe. As he walked past the entrance to the house he suddenly became aware of the silence and, like a premonition, he realized that the fresh earth had been laid on purpose to push the soldiers towards the house. In the instant of this thought, Kinton was thrown aside by an explosion. Two gas containers had been packed with explosives and left outside. Probably they had been detonated by someone watching the soldiers approach the house. It was that callous. A cloud of black smoke and debris swirled in the air. Nearby Sergeant Regan scrambled to his feet and saw a wounded Marine lying to his right. As the company medic, Regan went into action, despite his own injuries, packing and dressing the man's wounds, and with help from Kinton and the Marine brick commander he was made ready to board the Quick Reaction Force helicopter that had landed in a nearby field.

As the helicopter swept into the sky bound for Belfast hospital, the local school bell rang and the children poured out into the playground. Normal life existed in the midst of the fear and bloodshed. It was as if Crossmaglen operated two parallel lives and times. But where was that small brown dog?

After making sure the injured had received the necessary medical attention, Major Woodrow returned to the scene of the blast to walk the land. He was looking for clues that could lead to the bombers. It was the first day of the Grenadier Guards' tour and they had been involved in an ambush even before the handover had been completed. One Marine and a Guardsman lay in hospital – the Marine, named Weedon, later died of his wounds – and now the major had discovered a trail of blood. He knew it would not be human, as everyone had been accounted for. Could this be the blood of one of the unfortunate stray dogs that roamed the streets, ever hopeful of food? The trail died away to nothing.

Two days later Major Woodrow was making a routine visit to the medical hut when who should he see but the little brown dog that had accompanied the patrol on the day of the ambush. It transpired that he had been badly injured in the blast but had found his way back to the base where Sergeant Tim Fielding had found him lying just inside the perimeter fence. A dog lover and seasoned soldier, Fielding took the dog in his arms and carried him to the medical hut in the hope that the medic was equally fond of dogs. He found Sergeant Regan. Regan examined and stitched the hole in the dog's side and tended to the cuts on his ears. Patched, stitched and swathed in bandages the little dog was now more crêpe bandage than brown fur. But he was in safe hands and, probably for the first time in his life, he was somewhere he could genuinely call home.

Over the next four days the new recruit slept on his makeshift bed in the medical hut or on one of the bunks in the 18-man dormitory. He was not his usual perky self and for once showed little interest in what was happening around him. Fielding tended to the dog's every need but became very concerned when he refused to eat. Major Woodrow, a dog lover himself, recognized how close Fielding was becoming to the injured stray and how the dog's welfare was dominating his off-duty hours.

We could all see Fielding's determination to make Rat better. He virtually adopted the dog and made it his personal crusade to encourage him to take food. It was very touching to watch. And I think the dog, as much as a dog is able, realized the man wasn't going to give up and gradually Fielding's tender care started to pay off. Rat rallied round and was soon back on his rather weirdly shaped four legs.

Aware that taking the dog off the street could be a potential problem if he was a local family's pet, Major Woodrow conducted an investigation. The word on the street confirmed that the dog had been a stray for some time and showed no attachment to anyone, other than the soldiers. The company commander felt a sense of relief. He hadn't relished the idea of telling Fielding that the dog had to be expelled from the barracks. Clearly the little chap had already had a good effect on the men. He had once been their playful friend and now he had suffered as they were suffering. He had been injured in the line of duty with his fellow soldiers. He was to them, a soldier dog.

But to many of the men he had become something more than that. Major Woodrow recalls: 'In times of adversity you can confide in a dog in a way you feel you cannot in another human being for fear of being thought weak or stupid. Fortunately Rat was very sensitive to human emotion and so he saw your fear before you felt it. He was good for the men because he never judged anyone and he never failed to provide comfort when it was needed. It was good just to have him around.'

And so the British Army base in Crossmaglen adopted the scruffy little brown dog. That meant it was time to give him a name.

Although the dog came to be known as Rats, the Grenadier Guards who adopted him still insist that his name was Rat, in the singular. But everyone has their own version of why the choice of name. 'Rat seemed a good name for the dog but for many different reasons,' explains Major Woodrow. 'He will always be Rat to us because, quite simply, he looked like a rat. Also he was very dirty and had some filthy habits when we first met him. On top of that he liked chasing rodents in the barracks, which was very useful, although he was not overly successful and he was bitten more than once. Some will tell you that his name is short for "rations" and certainly this dog loved his food.'

As soon as he had made a full recovery Rat was allowed to wander where he liked. His priority on his first night out of hospital was to find a cosy bed. No one minded the dog sharing their bunk so he was given the choice of all 18. Rat took one look at the three tiers of brutally rigid accommodation and skipped jauntily past all of them, making a beeline for the single bed in the company commander's room, where he stopped briefly to relieve himself and then moved on. It was a good job the major took it in good humour. It helped that back home he was the proud owner of Willoughby, a basset hound, and understood the idiosyncrasies of canine behaviour; otherwise Rat would have had the shortest career ever in the British Army. But one thing was for sure, he had to have a bed he could call his own even if he preferred to share with Tim Fielding. No one wanted Rat leaving his calling card on their bed!

His life on the streets had made Rat greedy with food. If it was offered, Rat would eat it. What many of the men failed to appreciate was that Fielding took care of Rat. He fed and watered him and made sure the dog had no need to beg. But Rat couldn't help begging and the men wanted to share their chips and chocolate, their suet pudding and sweets and everything else that passed for food. It was probably how he acquired a liking for his favourite Army 'grub', the NAAFI's special steak pies. Unsurprisingly, someone was always clearing up after one of Rat's eating binges. 'He could be quite revolting,' recalls Major Woodrow. 'There were times when it seemed he was sick all the time and it was not one of his most endearing qualities. At Christmas when the fridge was full of goodies Rat just sat at the fridge door waiting for treats and, of course, he was never disappointed.'

The soldiers' time off duty could never be spent off the base. It was too dangerous. It was impossible for the men to walk into shops or pubs in a social capacity. It simply couldn't work that way. It was not because the locals generally wanted to be unfriendly; it was, on the whole, because they were afraid to be seen as anything else. A British soldier in Northern Ireland was just that, both on and off duty.

Everything the soldiers needed for their four or five months' tour of duty lay within the confines of the high steel and concrete walls of the base, fortified to keep those inside safe and the Opposition outside. Entertainment was in short supply and the men couldn't go out, so the company of a dog took on a special significance. It was Rat's bold cheekiness that warmed the hearts of the soldiers. His playfulness and eager expression lifted spirits and a few minutes watching Rat running around with his plastic toy duck and a few rounds of hide-the-sock were welcome entertainment. Having him there to sit with, talk to and just watch waddling around the barracks was invaluable. Many of the soldiers said that he made a kind of home where there was no other sign of home.

Thanks to Sergeant Fielding's care, Rat was now always well presented for duty, and a shampooed Rat was far more welcome in the dormitory than the dirty version the soldiers had first met. Sergeant Fielding remembers that his charge was never really that muddy, even for a dog whose stomach was so close to the ground. He somehow managed to skip over the worst of it, which was just as well because he was never keen on a bath. There was another plus point about the baths; the end result showed that Rat was really a very handsome dog. He wasn't a dull, matt brown colour at all but every shade of warm copper and rust. And underneath he was not a mucky cream but brilliant white with white socks to match. It didn't matter that after one patrol he was ready for the bath again! At least everyone could see he was cared for.

He lived the best of a dog's life and had the run of the base, but his territory was essentially the room Fielding and Regan shared and the rooms opposite that, which happened to be the Officers' Mess and the Operations Room. He was regularly found in this area of the base but if it was very cold, no one needed to look further than any of the gas fires on the camp. He loved the heat and would stay and soak it up until someone moved him along with their foot. But if they did that they were almost assured a lap companion for as long as they were prepared to keep still or put up with him rolling over for his tummy to be tickled.

He may have been a dog of very mixed ancestry but he had found a family now and they were proud to have him around.

Rat wasn't the only dog on the base. A black Labrador called Fleabus liked to hang around with Rat. Their favourite places included the helipad and lying together on Fielding's bunk. Another dog, Nutter, joined the team but he was more of a free agent and didn't get so close to the soldiers except when there was food around. Scruffy, a little white mongrel never made it into the base. For some reason, Rat kept Scruffy at tail's length as far as his inner circle was concerned. And so it happened that Rat built up his human and canine friends inside and outside the huge steel gates. But with all the dogs around it was Rat who attracted the most attention and affection. What did this small misshapen terrier have that the others did not?

To those who served alongside him it was simply that he was an 'everyman' dog. He was the ordinary soldier's dog. The kind of dog any of them could have had at home. He always met everyone with a smile and bright eyes and was always eager to join in. But the one thing that set Rat apart from the other dogs was his keenness to join the men on patrols. This made him one of them. It made him a soldier and one that faced all the dangers they faced. They admired his spirit as much as his intelligence and in all of that he was a huge boost to the troops' morale.

'It was quite a common sight to see Sergeant Fielding lean down and grab Rat in one hand and put him inside his jacket before heading out on duty,' recalls Major Woodrow.

Fielding wanted to take him and, quite honestly it was difficult for the man to escape without Rat scampering along at his heels. Others came to regard the dog as something of a lucky mascot so he was almost always welcome. For me, the dog's instinct and impeccable hearing could often be an asset to the patrol. Rat could hear the Opposition long before we did. If we saw them it was often too late.

The Dog that Saved My Life

Rat was intelligent and quick to learn anything Fielding or the others tried to teach him. Sometimes he worked situations out for himself and because he was almost always on patrol with Fielding or someone else he picked up some soldiers' behaviour. The men patrolled the streets and the countryside of South Armagh. The houses, streets and cars held their own menacing secrets and there was potentially a sniper in every window. The lush grass and thick hedges of the countryside presented a different fear of hidden mines and booby-trap bombs. Seeing the dog skipping confidently down the roads or through the country lanes was strangely comforting for the men. To see a dog looking so happy out walking, head held high and eyes bright with anticipation was as near to normal as anything could be. It was hard to admit the reality that each man, and the dog too, risked their life with every step they took.

Rat soon learnt that if the patrol came to a halt he should do the same. Dropping onto his belly, Rat would remain motionless until the order was given to move off. In the countryside he was aware of the need to be overly alert and acted only on the orders issued by the patrol commander. If the men stopped to eat, Rat would remain close by, watching out for them like a sentry on duty. If he wasn't being carried by Fielding or someone from another patrol then he would be waiting by the gates to the base in the hope that he could hitch a piece of the action with someone. He didn't like being left behind. But there were times when an operation demanded the utmost stealth and for that a dog could be unpredictable and therefore dangerous company. On one occasion during a night patrol Rat and Fleabus appeared uninvited. It was unusual to see Fleabus out of the camp and although Rat had some sense of the correct behaviour, Fleabus was quite a different matter. He was a big dog and therefore a danger in an area where mines were a possibility. Rat was light enough to skip over the ground but Fleabus could have not only jeopardized the exercise but endangered lives too. He had a habit of getting in the way around the cramped accommodation in the base and now he was in the way again.

Patrols and exercises in the field were part of every-day life for the soldiers stationed in Armagh. One night the men were making their way to a deserted farmhouse in the countryside outside Crosssmaglen where they were to spend the night. They left under the cover of darkness and as they approached the location a rustling noise in the undergrowth prompted the patrol to hit the ground. As the noise got louder the men raised their weapons and prepared to face the Opposition. However, out of the darkness appeared Rat and Fleabus. Rat wagged his tail and nuzzled the patrol commander, Sergeant Knight, in the hope of a pat on the head. Knight feared that the inexperienced Fleabus would bark a greeting. Furious with the dogs and fear-ful the operation would be discovered and men's lives lost, Knight decided to cancel the patrol, but before he could give the order he noticed Rat sniffing all over the ground ahead of them. He knew that if there were an ambush ahead the dogs would sniff it out and possibly bark a warning, so, until then, it could be assumed it was safe to move on towards the farmhouse. As they moved forward Rat and Fleabus worked the ground ahead and then ran back to the patrol. Each time they returned it proved the way ahead was clear of mines and the Opposition. With the dogs checking over such a wide area, Sergeant Knight was confident in moving forward to the target. When the men arrived safely the dogs took it upon themselves to leave and were not seen again until the patrol returned the next morning. Rat and Fleabus were waiting at the gates to greet them.

Rat never minded moving anywhere on four feet. His jaunty, skipping trot was part of his charm but it was not unusual to see his foxy tail and springy back legs disappear into the back of a Scarrycan. The Saracen armoured vehicle was the only car-like transport the Army used in Crossmaglen. Nothing else could be considered safe. Claustrophobic and lacking comfort, the Scarrycan was essential on patrols and one was always somewhere watching and waiting and protecting. For Rat, the sight of a Scarrycan meant one thing: a free ride. As long as there was a driver and a tea urn inside there was always room for a little dog to curl up on the other seat.

But Rat's real love was helicopters. If he couldn't leap into one the men would put him in an Army bag and he would be lifted aboard and let out so he could take up his position under the back seat. The danger time was jumping out. When transferring Army personnel into strategic positions the helicopter would hover to allow the men to jump out. Landing would leave it vulnerable. Rat was quick to learn the drill and as soon as he felt the helicopter go into a decent he would move forward to jump out. Three feet or thirty feet from the ground, it didn't matter; Rat was ready to go. Everyone and everything, including the domestic waste, went in and out of the Army base by helicopter. Despite being a large and obvious target for the Opposition, helicopters were still the best and the safest way to travel.

Sergeant Fielding was the first to take Rat into the air, just to see how he would get on. He knew Rat was fascinated by helicopters because he had watched how the dog reacted just watching them fly in and out of the base. He wouldn't run in and cause a problem but his fur would visibly bristle and his ears would prick up as soon as he heard a helicopter approach. And of course he heard that before any human being. Everyone could tell that Rat was curious about the helicopter but how would he like flying? Fielding knew there was only one way to find out so he gathered Rat in his arms and stepped into the helicopter. After a few moments of uncertainty Rat settled on Fielding's lap for the rest of the journey. He was never to give up his rides in the Scarrycan but helicopters became his new favourite way to travel.

Major Woodrow decided a daily aerial reconnaissance was a necessary addition to the regular foot patrols. After all, a helicopter could 'patrol' an area that would take days on foot, and considering the British Army had 300 miles along the border to survey and protect, helicopters were to prove invaluable. Fielding was pleased that Rat enjoyed riding in the air as much as travelling in the armoured vehicles as he really didn't want to leave the dog behind. He felt safer having Rat alongside him and many of the men felt the same too. Where there was a need to run both a foot patrol and a helicopter, Rat would follow Fielding. It went without saying.

One misty morning in January 1979 Major Woodrow was leading a helicopter patrol of the border as Fielding took a foot patrol over the same ground. Rat was at his heels. The dog had already lost half his tail in the firebomb attack but it had not put him off joining his friends. Easy to spot from the helicopter, a car and an open truck carrying a mortar base plate attracted the major's attention and he ordered a closer look. As the helicopter descended, the men in the vehicles opened fire. Receiving a radioed message from the helicopter, Fielding and the rest of the foot patrol commandeered two passing cars and raced to the scene to help their colleagues. The helicopter had been hit but the pilot had managed to keep it in the air. Rat ran out of the cars with his colleagues, baring his teeth at the gunmen. The suspects, outnumbered, reversed their vehicles and escaped south over the border. No one was hurt that day but 10 days later they were not so lucky. Once again a helicopter patrol commanded by Major Woodrow spotted a lorry and a van acting suspiciously and went in to take a look. It was a trap. Automatic rifles and machine guns battered the helicopter. The pilot was hit in the face with shrapnel and Major Woodrow sustained a number of gunshot wounds to his legs and was airlifted to Musgrave hospital in Belfast but not before he handed over to the new regiment on site. The soldiers managed to contain the damage but the helicopter was crippled by shots to the rotor blades as it made its way back to base.

I never saw Rat again, and I insist that he will always be Rat to the Grenadiers. I was airlifted to hospital after that and to be honest my mind was still on what we had just encountered and how the men were going to survive this and get back to duties. The Guards were to be posted to Germany next so there was no time to dwell. We did our job in Ireland. We did what we were there to do.

The Army never underestimated the Opposition. To those who were posted to Northern Ireland this was real soldiering. This was what all their training was about and a test of their ability to contain the activities of that formidable and unpredictable organization.

As the men of the Grenadiers prepared to follow their company commander out of the base Rat sensed something was wrong. Fielding recalls how the dog glued himself to his heels, almost afraid that the soldier would make a move without him. Rat was amongst heroes and with men who had not only served with him, they had saved his life. Keith Regan, who had saved Rat's life after the petrol-bomb attack, received the BEM for his service in Crossmaglen. Kevin Kinton had been injured several times during his tour of duty and for him the friendship of the little brown dog was something that helped keep him grounded: the dog was a touchstone for kindness amidst the hostility. For Fielding, the parting was particularly painful. Man and dog had become inseparable. At one point Fielding made plans to take Rat home to England, but that proved to be impossible as the battalion was to transfer to Germany soon after.

Rat was there to see the men take the helicopter out of the base. One by one they patted the dog's head before they boarded. As the last man stepped into the chopper Rat looked towards the door and began to run to it. 'I could tell Rat was going to try and leap into the helicopter and he wasn't always that good at it,' said Fielding. 'I had to pick him up and take him to the man who was taking over from me. I have no doubt at all that he knew we were leaving him and might never see any of us again. All I can say is that he had been a blessing to all of us while we were there. So far as any dog could, he had made us happy.' Rat whined and struggled to run after the helicopter. Fielding admitted that it 'almost broke my heart'.

Life with the Queen's Regiment was not the same as it had been with the Grenadiers for Rat. For a start he was called Rats, not Rat, and although that didn't bother him at all he was slow to attach himself to any one man. He went back to sleeping under bunks rather than lying in them and he drifted between the soldiers, perhaps looking for his old friends before he committed to making new ones. He was not quite the same dog, but then he was battle scarred, and maybe the ravages of the bullets, petrol bombs, shrapnel and other injuries acquired leaping in and out of helicopters and Scarrycans were having an effect. Or maybe it was the emotional strain of losing another group of friends and starting all over again.

But there were some of Rats's old habits that did not disappear with the Grenadiers. His liking for chasing cars was always going to be an accident waiting to happen. Vehicle checkpoints were always fun for Rats because cars were right there in front of him to chase. As soon as the soldiers had checked the car and it was driving away Rats would be there biting at the tyres. Most drivers realized he was there and moved away slowly, even though he followed them for a full 20 or 30 yards. But on one occasion, just after the arrival of the Queen's Regiment, Rats chased one car too many. He had watched the car as the soldiers checked it over and then, as usual, as the car moved away, he ran in towards the wheels. Suddenly the car veered to the left and Rats disappeared under it.

Yelping with pain the dog lay at the roadside. The soldiers saw what happened and dashed to Rats's side. Corporal Ainsworth gathered Rats up and ran with him back to base. The dog's left front leg was too damaged to be treated on site, and so the Queen's Regiment arranged a helicopter to fly Rats to Battalion HQ at Bessbrook. From there he was transferred to the Maze Prison at Long Kesh where a team of veterinary surgeons waited to examine the patient. Rats had a broken leg and was lucky to have escaped with only one serious injury. No one knows if the driver deliberately drove into Rats or if it was a genuine accident. That could never be proven but it was important to the soldiers that their mascot received the best of attention and within a month his leg was as good as new.

No sooner was Rats back on his feet than he was back to his old car-chasing antics. Maybe it would not have been so bad if he had limited his bad habits to chasing cars, because the day he chose to take on a bus was the day he needed stitches in his head. It was around this time that the RAF became reluctant to let him fly with them. They didn't want to be responsible for any injury to Rats. After all, he was becoming far too important to the base to risk that. Although he hadn't adopted any one particular friend amongst the men from the Queen's Regiment, they all played their part in making sure the little dog was well taken care of.

But there was one thing they had to change for their mascot – his passport to the skies. They knew how much he liked taking to the air and so they worked together to make sure that Rats was never left behind. No flight left without Rats being smuggling aboard inside someone's jacket or a Bergen (backpack).

'Rats was a member of the company so we were not going to leave him behind. If we were going somewhere, Rats was going too,' recalls Major (now Colonel) Richard Graham, the company commander. 'When you are in a situation where you are surrounded by adversity, a small item of happiness can take on huge significance. Rats was a small trace of happiness in adversity and for that he was very important to all of us.'

When the 1st Battalion Queen's Own Highlanders arrived in Crossmaglen in August 1979 so did Corporal Joseph O'Neil. He was a Catholic and a family man and his tour of Northern Ireland had begun as his wife was about to have their third child. O'Neil had concerns about being in one of the most dangerous locations for any British serviceman at this time in his life but it was his job and, of course, he was just going to get on with it. But it was the sight of Rats waiting to greet the advance party from the helicopter that interested O'Neil. He wasn't expecting to see a dog in this God-forsaken place. For some reason the appearance of a small dog stuck in his mind and the next time he saw Rats, he was sleeping on the empty bunk of one of the corporals who had flown out that day. The man had played the mouth organ and other soldiers had said how Rats had liked the sound and often tried to join in, 'singing' along. O'Neil couldn't play anything but he tried to entice Rats with a whistle. 'Come on little fella ... it's alright ... come over here.' To the soldier's surprise, Rats followed the sound of the whistle and settled on O'Neil's bunk. It wasn't really the soldier's intention to invite the dog to take over his bunk but it was too late, Rats had moved in.

By the morning Rats was on patrol at O'Neil's feet, tugging at his bootlaces and never moving more than a few inches from the soldier at any one time. 'It seems you've chosen me as your friend after all,' observed O'Neil, who was already missing his family. 'To many of us, having Rats around was like having a child in the camp. He was funny. He made us laugh and if he chose you for company he could be a comfort just sitting on a lap or running at heel on patrol. The dog was our friend and we were grateful for it.'

The Highlanders lost five men during that particular tour of Northern Ireland. A remote-controlled bomb killed one soldier in Crossmaglen Square; two were killed when a helicopter was shot down and two more died in an ambush at Warrenpoint along with 16 other British troops. This attack coincided with the assassination of Lord Mountbatten on holiday in the Republic and the world's media suddenly was concentrating on the trouble in Northern Ireland. Death and misery had been features of daily life on the front line of this conflict for 10 years but the high-profile activity that culminated in the death of a member of the Royal family brought the world's focus on Crossmaglen. BBC television cameras descended on the Army base to capture the essence of the Troubles. It didn't take long for them to be introduced to Rats.

The troops that had served with Rats at their heels did not need to be told of the dog's value as a friend and mascot. They had experienced it first hand but this was not an aspect of Army life that the outside world was aware of. The significance of a small brown dog was known only to the soldiers and their families. Letters home told of the dog's antics and how he played games and brought some light relief to the soldiers' lives. In that way he was a comfort to those left worrying at home too. At least they knew there was a welcome diversion from the soldiers' constant fear. There was a dog called Rats.

Maybe it needed the arrival of a television crew to highlight Rats's contribution to life on the base or maybe it was something the soldiers had planned all along, but this dog was about to be honoured for his loyalty, his friendship and his ability to raise morale amidst all the conflict. A medal, made from a dog disk, was struck in his honour. On one side there was the Queen's head and on the other his name and Army number: Delta 777 – Delta for Delta Company (after the company he was serving with) and the triple seven because it was considered the luckiest number possible. It was suspended from a red and white ribbon, and was the Army's way of recognizing Rats as a 'soldier dog'; and like all soldiers who are awarded medals, Rats was guest of honour at a special ceremony. As a piper played 'Scotland the Brave', the company sergeant major pinned the medal to the dog's collar. It was a poignant moment for O'Neil and one he was forced to share with millions of people watching on television. Even O'Neil's young sons saw 'Daddy's dog' on the television and pleaded with him to bring Rats home to Glasgow.

O'Neil, like several other soldiers who had served with Rats, was desperate to take the dog home at the end of his tour of duty but by this time the dog was part of the base. Despite encouragement from his friends O'Neil knew that he couldn't smuggle Rats out in his kit bag, although he would have dearly loved to. He could not be the one to take this hero dog out of Crossmaglen. But it was time for the Highlanders to move out and for Rats to lose another friend, someone else he had grown close to. This happened every four or five months. Suddenly the person Rats had chosen as his friend was gone, never to be seen again. To try and avoid the tearful farewell at the base it was decided to fly Rats to HQ in Bessbrook. The location made no difference. The farewell was just as tearful, for man and dog. Rats whined and, to the men, it sounded like crying. Twice he ran after O'Neil as walked towards the Army lorry that was to take the men away. Twice the soldier brought him back, the second time handing him to the man who was going to take over the care of the soldier dog of Crossmaglen.

Major Vyvyan Harmsworth, Company Commander 1st Battalion the Welsh Guards, had first heard about Rats during a period of pre-Northern Ireland training several months earlier. A Grenadier Guards officer had shown him a picture of the regiment in Crossmaglen and one of the men was holding a scruffy looking dog. The dog was introduced as Rat and the message was: 'When you get out there you must look after the little chap.' And who was he? 'He's a mascot and a marvellous little dog.' Major Harmsworth did not forget the request and when he met Rats in the flesh he could understand why the Guards had been so insistent that the dog was well looked after. 'From the moment we arrived in Crossmaglen it was obvious that Rats was clearly a boost to the men's morale. It was well known that he had been shot at, blown up, run over and injured in a firebomb attack. In other words, he had been through hell, the same as the men and that is why they not only had great affection for the dog, they respected him too. He was, to them, another soldier. A friend.'

The man O'Neil handed Rats over to, Corporal Arwel Lewis, part of the Welsh Guards' advance party of NCOs. He was with the anti-tank platoon, which for this tour was attached to the three platoons already in the Prince of Wales Company. There was a need for additional manpower to face the Opposition as by this time, October 1979, the death toll of British soldiers in Northern Ireland had reached 60. Lewis had already been on his first patrol in Crossmaglen, with Joseph O'Neil leading the way and alongside him the ever-present Rats. Lewis had grown up on a farm in North Wales and was used to dogs so, for him, the sight of the scruffy brown mongrel skipping ahead of the soldiers was a welcome sight. It was Lewis's introduction to the man and dog duo and it was a meeting that showed O'Neil that his dog would be in safe hands. Just a few days later O'Neil was handing Lewis the dog for safe-keeping.

Whether it was because Corporal Lewis was used to dogs or just because Rats instantly liked the man is immaterial; the important thing for Rats was that they were instant friends. 'He was always smiling,' recalls Lewis. 'He bobbed along at my heels when we were on patrol and every now and again he would look up at me as if to check that I was OK. It's his facial features I remember more than anything else, not his stumpy tail or his scarred ears but the way he looked at me and how we hit it off right away. He was always cheerful. Nothing got him down.'

He patrolled with the Welsh Guards, ate with them and slept in their bunks and everyone liked him. There wasn't a thing he could do wrong, except go out and not come back for ages. As a rule Rats preferred to stay close to Lewis and that was the case whether he was on patrol or enjoying some rest and recuperation on the base. But every now and again he would be tempted to hitch a ride on a helicopter and then another and another until he had no idea where he was. If he arrived late at night it wasn't unusual for the soldiers, wherever he landed, to feed him and put him up for the night. If he found himself at HQ in Bessbrook the men would find him a bunk, and next morning a genuine 'dog's breakfast', including plenty of sausages, would be prepared in the cookhouse especially for him. Once fed, Rats would head for the helipad where he would be put on a helicopter bound for Crossmaglen. Several could come in from the various base camps along the border so the men would help him out by shouting and pointing at the right helicopter for his return journey. 'That's your helicopter Rats. Off you go.' Maybe there was a particular noise from the engine or maybe it was down to perfect dog sense no one could fathom out, but somehow he knew when the chopper was about to land at his 'stop'.

The dog was known by everyone, everywhere and so when he went walkabout everyone knew to contact Crossmaglen, and then Corporal Lewis would inevitably be sent to collect him. On one occasion Rats went missing and everyone on the base noticed his absence, even Major Harmsworth. Without wasting time he ordered Corporal Lewis to track the dog down and collect him from wherever he had landed. After doing some detective work Lewis discovered that Rats had travelled to Bessbrook and was having his usual 'dog's breakfast' of bacon, eggs and extra sausage. Lewis caught the next flight out. Very often Rats travelled alone but not without the base sending a message ahead. It was not unusual to receive messages like this:

Rats arriving your destination five minutes stop Turn him round, give him a kick up backside and send him back.

Thanks to the visit from the BBC cameras Rats was becoming a household name. Visitors to the Army base in Crossmaglen wanted to meet the little dog with the huge profile and would ask for him by name. It could get a little embarrassing if Rats had decided to absent himself for the day. If he disappeared for more than a few hours the men would become concerned and begin calling round to track him down. Rats's love of heli-copters was usually to blame. With over 50 flights a day moving through Battalion HQ to bases along the front line on the border it was a great temptation for him to jump aboard with soldiers heading out on patrol. Rats thought this was great fun and the perfect escape from the confines of the base.

If he went AWOL for longer than expected and there was not a whisker of a clue to his whereabouts it was time to set up a search party. This wasn't illogical thinking or wasting soldiers' time: this was the men looking after one of their own. 'When you are in a hostile environment the Opposition will look for any way it can to intimidate or disturb you,' recalled Major Woodrow of the Grenadiers. 'When I was in Belfast it was not unusual for soldiers on patrol to find one of the strays they had befriended, dead and hung on a wall. This was what we were dealing with all the time. This was the level the Opposition operated on. It was no wonder we feared for Rat's safety.'

On the streets Rats received the same treatment as the soldiers – indifference. Children could be unpredictable but by the time the Welsh Guards were on patrol the atmosphere had become slightly less aggressive and it was the children, above all, who warmed to the sight of the soldiers and the dog together. But their attitude could change daily: one day they would stroke Rats, and the next give him a sly kick. Unsurprisingly, Rats's attitude could be ambivalent too. He was a soldier dog and a lover of the uniform so if he saw a civilian hurt his friends they became his sworn enemy. He protected those who cared for him and he proved time and time again that he was so determined not to leave their side that he literally put his life on the line alongside them. Maybe he knew that they would do the same for him.

Rats's fame began to spread. His appearances on television and in the newspapers always brought new fans who couldn't resist sending their good wishes and gifts to this little star of Northern Ireland. It was not unusual for Rats to receive the bulk of the incoming mail at the Army base. Children sent him toys and their pocket money and pensioners sent their savings with written requests to buy Rats special treats to eat, and warm blankets for his bed. He was the most effective public-relations vehicle the Army could have hoped for at a time when the Troubles were at their height. This was an Irish stray, adopted by British soldiers, turned media-created icon and a symbol of survival.

By the end of 1979, Rats was more than a local hero: he was an international celebrity, and this time it was thanks to the charity Pro-Dogs and its founder, the late Lesley Scott-Ordish. Awarded the charity's Gold Medal and crowned Dog of the Year, Rats, once again, stepped into the limelight and this time he took Corporal Lewis and Major Harmsworth with him. When news broke of the award Corporal Lewis was despatched with Rats, Guardsman Parry and two police officers in an unmarked police car to Belfast for a flight to London. They were on their way to a television interview on the BBC programme, *Nationwide*. Rats stayed at Corporal Lewis's side, even in make-up, where he made more new friends who couldn't help fussing over the little hero. Then it was off to a London hotel for the medal ceremony. The medal citation read: 'For Valour and Devotion to Duty and for the comfort provided to soldiers serving in Crossmaglen'. It was every soldier's sentiments exactly. The men agreed that no dog was more deserving of this honour than Rats.

On 9 December 1979, the Gold Medal on its tartan ribbon was placed around Rats's neck. He gave a bark of thanks and sniffed the other gift, a bone wrapped in silver foil. Not a great fan of normal dog food, Rats decided to leave the bone and save his appetite for the delights of Army food when he returned to barracks in Crossmaglen. Even the dinner following the presentation did not entice Rats to eat, and neither could Corporal Lewis who was sitting next to him. Despite his lack of appetite Rats was his usual cheerful self and he joined in each round of applause with a loud bark. He had been showered specially for the occasion and sparkled before the cameras. This dog was unafraid to face life on the streets of one of the most dangerous places in the world so he was not going to shy away from flash photography as the world's media gathered to see this Dog of the Year.

The following day was spent on a photoshoot around London, taking in all the famous landmarks. Rats had to stay on a lead the whole time to stop him running away or, more likely, chasing cars. A flight back to Belfast and then on to Crossmaglen brought the soldiers and the dog back to base.

As he travelled back home via Belfast, Rats suffered a bout of car sickness. That wasn't entirely unusual but his bloodshot eyes and downcast look were. Something was wrong. Major Harmsworth arranged for Lewis to take Rats directly to the Army Dog Unit at Long Kesh where the veterinary surgeon was able to attend to him. It appeared that Rats had been bitten by a rat and was suffering the consequences. It would take a small operation and a few days' rest and recuperation to put Rats back on his feet again. But for a dog at the top of his Army career there was no time to lie around. His public awaited him.

Rats was now receiving between 200 and 300 letters a day and gifts galore! Media coverage of the medal ceremony had reminded people of this dog's service in Northern Ireland and his value to the men on the front line. Each letter that was received was answered by a member of the Welsh Guards and a Rats paw print signed each one. As the parcels arrived, Rats was allowed to sniff through each one and out of everything, including the many Christmas cakes, leads, collars, bones and treats, he chose a squeaky duck as his favourite toy. He received two jackets from HQ in Bessbrook – a combat jacket to wear on patrols and a red ceremonial jacket bearing the insignia of the Welsh Guards. Despite many gifts of comfortable dog beds and pillows, Rats still preferred to sleep at the bottom of Corporal Lewis's bunk. It seemed that old habits died hard for this war dog. 'Rats was used to the simple pleasures of Army cooking and a dormitory bunk. Despite the many gifts and treats his favourite playtime was with an old sock and his favourite activity of all was being out on patrol with the men,' said Corporal Lewis. 'He was a great comfort and a character and such a huge boost to morale. He was always cheerful and nothing got him down. We admired the old dog for that.'

As the Christmas excitement and media frenzy calmed down it became clear that Rats was unwell. He was still managing his three meals a day and the odd side helping of steak where he could, but there was something not quite right. He was still eager to leap into helicopters though, and he had his own posse of stray dogs to lead around the town. 'I thought it was very funny to see Rats lead his patrol of dogs down the street as we were leading a patrol. It was as if he was mimicking us after so long serving with us,' said Lewis. 'But his love of chasing cars was always something we hated and it was always in the back of our minds that he could take that bad habit too far.'

One night, not long after Christmas, Rats was out on the streets with his gang of strays when a car came careering down the road and appeared to swerve towards the dogs. Rats was oblivious to what was going on as he was, as usual, absorbed in what he was doing. But a nearby patrol watched as the car ran over one of the dogs and sped off into the night. At first it looked as if Rats had been killed but it was his friend Scruff who was the victim that day. The men who watched the incident were convinced that it was deliberate; after all there was a bounty on Rats's head. His popularity with the soldiers and public had made him a target for the Opposition, and he was lucky to survive this time.

It was for these two very good reasons that Major Harmsworth and the Welsh Guards began to think of Rats's retirement. They did not want to restrict his love of patrolling with the men or taking his place on the helicopters because they believed that would be cruel, but it wasn't safe to let him carry on. In a way the veterinary surgeon at Long Kesh made the decision easier: Rats was feeling the effects of his old injuries and it was time to stop. And so the decision was taken to medically retire Rats, for his own health and safety.

In dog years, Rats was somewhere in his late fifties, and X-rays showed that his battle scars included 12 pieces of shrapnel in his little body and various bumps and bruises gained from collisions with vehicles and free-falling from helicopters. Although Rats refused to give in to his body slowing down, it was slowing and one more misjudged leap from a helicopter or one more attempt to dodge a sniper's bullet could be the last. This hero deserved something better than that. But not before the Welsh Guards had said a fond farewell to the Retiring Member of the Regiment with all the pomp and ceremony they could muster.

It was on a chill April morning in 1980 that soldier dog Delta 777 bowed out of the Army after a distinguished career. At the time of his retirement Rats was the longest-serving British soldier in Northern Ireland. The parade ground at Pirbright in Surrey glistened with gold brocade highlighting the scarlet tunics of the Prince of Wales's Company, 1st Battalion, the Welsh Guards. Accompanied by a personal escort and an honour party of four guardsmen, the guest of honour moved forward. The waddle of a walk, the bristling rust-coloured coat and the tinkling of medal on metal heralded the approach of a veteran dog soldier on parade for one last time. Overhead the rumble of a helicopter broke the silence and caught the attention of the Retiring Member. He stopped, looked to the sky and pricked up his ears. Rats picked up a trot as he headed towards the flying beast. With all his old friends there to see him off and wish him well Rats timed his run perfectly and launched himself into the helicopter for the last time. Soldiers with many years' service under their belt and with images of comrades killed and injured still running in their heads said goodbye to their mascot dog of Cross-maglen with tears in their eyes. This giant amongst mascots had done his time and served loyally and with honour, and richly deserved his special place in so many hearts.

Rats retired from the British Army and lived another nine happy years with Major Harmsworth and his family in Kent. At the time the location had to be kept a secret to protect the dog from potential harm. Rats remained an IRA target for the rest of his life but it did not stop him enjoying a full and happy retirement as a family pet. He also managed to keep engagements as a canine celebrity, meeting Her Majesty the Queen and the Queen Mother, who were both keen to learn that Rats was enjoying his life in peacetime as much as his life in the Army.

'Rats adapted very well to life as a family dog,' said Major Harmsworth, 'but you could never drain away some of his Army living. He remained helicopter-minded, rushing to the top of the hill each time he heard one in the sky. I felt quite sorry when I saw the look of expectancy on his face as if it was going to land just for him.' So why was this little dog so important to the soldiers in Northern Ireland? What made him so special to so many? 'I think it was partly because he was a guy you could talk to,' said Major Harmsworth. 'We lost a Guardsman on that tour of Northern Ireland and Rats sensed the sadness, our grief. He was good at keying in to human emotion. He was also a constant in an environment that was as uncertain as shifting sand. Rats was solid. He was there for every man.'

Rats passed away in his sleep. Major Harmsworth found him curled up peacefully in his basket. He was buried in the garden of the family home where a gravestone still stands to honour the life of this extraordinary dog, of no particular breed, who had so much to give to all and always with a smile. A true soldier's friend.

Bonnie –

DOG is GOD Spelt Backwards

'When a dog becomes the person you trust most in the world, you know your life is in safe hands.'

(Corporal Jenny Chester, Royal Army Veterinary Corps)

I think about Bonnie every day. She's in my head wherever I am and whatever I'm doing. I could be shopping or cleaning the car or getting kitted out to work with my new partner, Casper, a narcotics sniffer dog, and Bonnie's big old Labrador face will appear ... smiling at me. If that sounds a bit crazy then I'm sorry but I spent four years with Bonnie at my side and in that time we got to know each other pretty well. We shared food when alone, a sleeping bag in the cold and in the heat we shared the shade of the same tree. We faced danger on the roadside and dodged bullets in the street. Ours was a friendship made for life.

Jenny Chester had wanted to join the Army from the moment she saw her big brother in his uniform. She thought he looked so smart and the exciting stories he had to share made her want to be part of it all. She wanted to be able to make their parents proud too and so, from the age of 14 her career path was set: to follow in her brother's military footsteps. By the time she reached 17 Jenny had dabbled with the idea of becoming a vet, but just as quickly had discounted the idea when she imagined the times she couldn't help a patient. Helping them heal was one thing, but having to put them to sleep was quite another. A career in the Army working with animals was the logical answer, so Jenny left the family home in Kent and joined up.

Dogs had featured in many of Jenny's earliest childhood memories. There had always been a dog or dogs in the house, and out of the many the family adopted over the years it was a Border collie called Judy who found herself a place in Jenny's heart. With traditional black-and-white colouring, soft brown eyes and an ever-alert expression, Judy was Jenny's constant companion from the age of four, and was always ready to walk a million miles at the drop of a hat. This dog rarely sat still but when she did it was never far from the biscuit barrel, although she would only eat biscuits if dunked in tea first.

Judy was 18 when she died. Jenny had grown up with the collie at her side so it was no wonder that this was the dog she measured every other one against. To Jenny, Judy was the perfect canine friend: always there when she was needed, always able to sense when Jenny needed the comfort of her head on her lap. To suddenly not have her around was very painful for Jenny. Then and there, aged 14, she made the decision always to have a dog in her life.

Army life suited Jenny and the three months of basic training passed relatively quickly. Within no time she was on her way to the Defence Animal Centre, Dog Training School in Melton Mowbray in Leicestershire. She was now just hours away from meeting her first AES (Arms and Explosives Search) dog – the dog who would be her partner, if all went well, for the next few years. Jenny felt a surge of excitement mixed with a little anxiety at the prospect. The induction process and the paperwork seemed to take forever. Settling in to the accommodation, drawing new kit and getting to know the other new recruits was all part of the excitement, but where was the dog?

The matching of handler and dog is similar in a way to an arranged marriage. By the time Jenny met her dog the Army had already done its homework and reached a decision on the best dog for her. But Jenny knew nothing about this dog – only that it would almost certainly be a Labrador. In reality not one of the recruits knew a thing until a list appeared on the notice-board in the mess that Monday evening. Jenny eagerly checked it for her name on the AES dog assignment list. It read: 'AES dogs to be assigned as follows: … Private Jenny Chester – Bonnie …'

'I couldn't wait for morning to come,' recalled Jenny. 'I felt like a kid on Christmas Eve. Silly really for a grown woman but I can't deny it, I was excited. I wanted to meet this dog. I wanted to get to work and live out my dream. And I had a vivid mental picture of this dog.' From the moment Jenny was told her dog's name was Bonnie she started working on a mental picture of an adorable Labrador, a big, playful puppy just like the one on the toilet roll adverts, all kisses and cuddles when off duty and totally loyal and attentive when on duty. According to Jenny, Bonnie was, of course, going to be the best AES dog ever, and by the time she reached the kennels she was more than ready to meet this 'wonder dog'.

Tuesday morning arrived. Rows and rows of dogs met Jenny and the seven other trainees as they stepped through the doors to the kennels. And what a welcome! A thousand decibels of eager, barking dogs, a hefty stink of disinfectant and a whiff of 'dog' grabbed everyone by the nostrils. Jenny smiled. She knew this was a smell she would have to get used to as it was going to be greeting her every day for some years to come. Taking a good look around Jenny could see the springer spaniels, German shepherds and a selection of Labradors all looking eager and friendly. Perhaps it was the sight of the uniforms that made the dogs so excitable, or maybe it was the fact that Jenny and her fellow trainees were the new kids on the block. As they were escorted through the kennel block Jenny quickly scanned the many faces staring out at her and wondered which dog was destined for her.

'Private Chester, your dog's over there.' Jenny looked to where the sergeant was pointing and there was a big, fit, smiley Labrador. It was love at first sight. 'Hello Bonnie,' said Jenny, extending her hand for Bonnie to sniff. No sooner had Jenny said her name than this cuddly dog was rolling over to show her tummy, lapping up the attention.

Dog and handler spent the rest of the morning together walking, playing and getting to know each other. 'As we sat together and then played catch and tug of war with the few toys she had in her kennel, I started to imagine how this partnership would work out. It felt so good and I remember hitting my bunk that night just knowing that I had the perfect dog for the job. I called my family to tell them all about Bonnie. I couldn't have been happier. I just knew the next few weeks we were to spend getting to know each other were going to be a doddle.'

Next morning Jenny was up early to see Bonnie and take her out for a walk, and to start the series of exercises which culminated in a passing-out parade in 15 weeks' time. By the time Jenny had Bonnie on her leash she was feeling pretty confident. Just 10 minutes later, Bonnie seemed to have suffered a personality change.

The dog that had been super-friendly and easy to please was suddenly the most stubborn canine on the planet. Everything Jenny asked her to do, the Labrador ignored or performed in slow motion. Right there and then Jenny felt she was the butt of a cruel joke. She was convinced that someone had swapped her Bonnie for some dog from hell.

Out of the corner of her eye Jenny could see the trainers looking at each other: they were smiling. What was so funny? Certainly Jenny couldn't see anything to laugh about. It turned out that Bonnie had something of a history. Jenny was not her first handler; she was her third in the last few months. Like the other seven dogs on the course Bonnie was a fully trained AES dog but she didn't have a handler. If she didn't make it this time with this handler it would be the end of the line for her, at least in that role. Jenny and Bonnie had to make it, for Bonnie's sake.

Jenny wondered if this stubborn dog's 'Miss Stroppy' ways had been her downfall all along. Certainly her 'Miss Oh So Cute' act one minute and her 'You must be joking I'm not doing that' attitude the next had not done her any favours so far. She wouldn't listen to a word Jenny said and although she knew there had to be a reason for the dog's behaviour, it was something that had to wait for now. Both had to get through the next three months of training and it was not going to be the doddle Jenny thought. This was going to be uphill all the way for dog and handler.

Bonnie had already proved herself a good AES dog. She had shown she had the skill and determination required for the job. Jenny, as a handler, had to show the same in equal proportions. The two had to work in partnership to create the kind of bond built on absolute trust – the trust needed to do the job.

The training Bonnie had gone through to become an AES dog was based on modern reward-based training techniques. The focus of the rewards was the humble tennis ball. To be able to find a specific item or substance a dog must first be exposed to its scent. Each time the dog locates that particular scent it indicates a 'find' by standing still. A find is rewarded with what becomes the dog's favourite plaything – a tennis ball.

Bonnie and Jenny were now being put to the test as a partnership. To pass out as a proficient AES team they would have to locate successfully weapons, explosives, ammunition and bomb-making equipment hidden in various locations, as they would have to for real in the field: in houses, factories, on roadsides and all kinds of outdoor terrain. In the next 15 weeks together they had to prove that they could work as an effective partnership, but Bonnie was not going to make it easy.

The first exercise was to search a large factory area, Bonnie and Jenny taking the upper level. Bonnie happily sniffed and swaggered her way up the staircases to the top level of the concrete maze of a building without any bother at all. But when she reached the railings at the top she just couldn't help having a laugh. 'She walked to the railings, looked at me and then popped her head through the bars,' recalled Jenny. 'I could tell she thought it was funny and of course she didn't do it once, she did it a few times before she realized that I was not amused. At one point she looked as if she was going to go through the bars and jump over and I would not have been surprised if she had. She was behaving like a naughty girl and I felt like a frustrated parent.'

Jenny was just 18 years old but she was starting to get the measure of this cheeky black Labrador. Bonnie was out to embarrass, there was no doubt about it and Jenny was convinced the dog wanted to put her in her place. It was probably something she had tried with her previous handlers. But Jenny wasn't about to give up. She had wanted to do this job for a long time and, besides, she liked Bonnie. She liked the dog's personality and spirit and thought Bonnie deserved another chance. Though Jenny was prepared to give all it took, was Bonnie going to return the commitment?

The road search was the next test. This time the smiling Labrador was raring to go. She sat patiently and obediently at Jenny's feet waiting for the order to move out. A road search involves the dog working at a distance ahead of the handler. The dog should move steadily up and down both sides of the road – up the left, across and then down the right to the handler, moving forward all the time. Bonnie was doing well with this exercise. Her head was down and her nose was stuck like glue to the roadside. Jenny was just beginning to think that the first sessions with her new dog were one-offs and this was the real Bonnie. But then, without warning, the dog spotted something in the middle of the road and veered off towards it. As Jenny came closer she could see that it was a dead badger and Bonnie was rolling over it. Squirming around in sheer delight Bonnie looked every inch a playful puppy rather than a four-year-old dog with a career in the Army. Once more, Bonnie had let herself down; Jenny had to collect her dog, stinking of badger, from the middle of the road.

Bonnie was shaping up to be a nightmare dog. All Jenny could see on the horizon was failure, and the more she thought about it the more convinced she became that she would fail alongside Bonnie and that would mean the end of her dream too. If Bonnie didn't pull something out of the bag very soon both of them would be looking for alternative careers. Bonnie had one last chance to prove to Jenny and to the commanding officer, Major Chris Ham, that she could do this job. And if she was going to make it she had to complete all the remaining tasks.

What happened to Bonnie that day Jenny had no idea at all, but it was as if she heard everything everyone was saying, and realized this next task was going to be either her finest hour or her final attempt. Jenny held her breath as she took off Bonnie's lead and put on the harness that signalled the start of the dog's working day. If all went well, Bonnie would have only one more task to perform, searching a house. But Jenny knew it could go either way and it didn't help her confidence at all.

Bonnie didn't put her nose or a foot wrong that day and seemed to take pleasure in showing Jenny how it was done. Jenny was so proud of her she hugged her for what seemed like an hour solid. All the time the words of the trainers echoed in her ears: 'You are a good team.' They saw that Bonnie knew the drill and what she was doing and had the best nose on her. It was not the write-up Jenny was expecting at all. Over the previous 12 weeks, Bonnie had done anything but prove she was a highly skilled explosives search dog.

'Instead of waiting for my next posting I thought I would be waiting for the train home.' But that day Bonnie proved to her new handler and to everyone around them that the best is always worth waiting for.

Jenny believed that Bonnie behaved in such an awkward and frustrating way to start with because she didn't find the tasks challenging enough for her. She wasn't stupid at all. She was quite the opposite and, like a bored child, she cranked up the awkwardness. When good behaviour was required, Bonnie delivered it. None of the others on the course thought Bonnie would complete the passing-out exercises but she did, and she did it with flying colours.

Bonnie's success was Jenny's licence to travel to Germany. The pair went there for another course and it was another chance for Bonnie to show off her skills. Germany is a regular stop-off for dogs serving with the Royal Army Veterinary Corps, like Bonnie. The dogs serving with the troops overseas have their respite breaks in Germany and those returning to the UK are quarantined there too. Jenny could feel her confidence in her dog grow by the day. She then understood her a little better too. She came to see how very intelligent Bonnie was but also how very funny, and as long as that dog humour was not misplaced in the front line it was a real asset to any team. There was no better accolade than being told you're a good team, and that was enough to tell Jenny they were on their way. And that meant on their way to Bosnia.

* * *

The conflict in Bosnia and Herzegovina, part of the former Republic of Yugoslavia, was a complex affair in which over 100,000 civilians and soldiers were killed and 1.8 million people were cruelly displaced. The core of the trouble was its historically multi-ethnic state, comprising Bosniaks, Serbs and Croats, and the ambitions of nationalists both in Bosnia and in the neighbouring republics of Serbia and Croatia. International armed conflict was sparked in March 1992 and continued until 1995. In 2005, the US Congress declared that 'the Serbian policies of aggression and ethnic cleansing meet the terms defining genocide.' As of early 2008, 45 Serbs, 12 Croats and 4 Bosniaks had been convicted of systematic war crimes in the Balkan wars of the 1990s.

It was into this confusion that Jenny and Bonnie arrived in November 2003 as part of the United Nations peace-keeping force.

Jenny remembered being told to pack lots of winter clothing as temperatures in Bosnia can reach as low as minus 20°C. 'When I heard that, I wondered why I had been so eager to utter the words: "You want volunteers for Bosnia? We'll go."' She couldn't help thinking that Bonnie might be cursing her the moment she took one breath of that cold air too. It was going to be hard on the dogs – any extreme temperature is – but for the moment Bonnie was happy; she could sense something was happening and she always liked that. Jenny was looking forward to it for many reasons. It would give her time to bond with Bonnie, and this deployment would test their skills as professionals and as a working team.

Bonnie didn't move far from Jenny's side on the day they left. Maybe they had been together long enough for her to know that Jenny was her handler and that it was comforting for Jenny to know she felt that way. Bosnia was going to be a great adventure for both of them and it was going to start on the plane out for Jenny. She had never flown before and just hoped this wasn't her turn to embarrass Bonnie. When you handle a dog, the dog is your priority the whole time, and Jenny didn't really have time to think about how she felt as there was so much kit to assemble, and settling Bonnie into her small travelling kennel looked as if it could be a real challenge too. But it was then that Jenny realized that Bonnie was the true professional here. Even if she didn't know the drill for flying she carried it off with confidence and that took the stress away from her new handler. As Bonnie, the only dog on the flight, was put in the hold and Jenny took her place for the journey, the rest of the handlers took their places in the huge transporter. It was like sitting in a giant flying cave.

It was lucky for Jenny that Bonnie slept all the way through the journey; some of the other handlers were not so fortunate. Jenny gave Bonnie an extra pat to let her know how pleased she was with her behaviour.

As the handlers gathered all their gear together to disembark they could see a deputation of fellow dog handlers waiting to greet them. This was Zagreb airport.

Jenny had heard so much about this place and now here she was, on her way to join the peace-keeping force in a country that was experiencing the closest Jenny had come to a war zone, in the middle of the night. She couldn't help wondering what she was doing! Sitting on the plane she had felt anxious, as no doubt everyone else did. But the good thing about having a dog to take care of is that everyone can divert their attention to the dog and that's always useful in times of stress. And dogs seem to understand. Certainly Bonnie did just that.

Jenny guessed it wasn't the end of their journey and she was right. The other handlers warned there was an hour's bumpy ride in an Army truck ahead of them. They were heading for the American-run part of Zagreb airport and then travelled on to Banja Luka metal factory, a base run by the British, where they would be sharing their canine and human accommodation.

But first Jenny had to release Bonnie from her lacon (the name for the Army travelling kennel) and give her a run after the journey. This was Jenny's first glimpse outside and Bosnia looked grey. She could smell the cold. 'There was a slightly metallic air that stung my face and then I could feel it creep through my clothes. All those people who told me to wrap up warm were not joking. The cold was overpowering. By night, it all looked and felt so strange. As we set off on the last lap of the journey I was looking forward to a good night's sleep and seeing my new "home" in the morning.'

The greyness of Bosnia by night had lingered into the morning. Cold mist covered every building and it looked as if it was there to stay. Jenny headed for the dog kennels, which were located at the other end of the base. She had been told the base was on the site of an old metal factory that had been converted into a self-contained military village. She could see the offices, restaurant, heli pads, newsagent and what looked like other shops. It was all built on the 'square' of the original building, which had been covered in metal cladding, probably in an attempt to brighten everything up. It didn't work as it was a very dismal building. But then, it didn't need to be anything else. Inside the factory, the heavy machinery had been dismantled and had been replaced by metal containers, originally designed to be portable offices but converted into sleeping accommodation known as 'Corrimecs', a little like Portakabins. Each contained a bed, a window at the end and, if you were lucky, a heater. Bonnie's kennel looked similar but it was smaller and the heating was better! It was all very bare and basic but it was going to be Jenny and Bonnie's home for the next six months.

Jenny's first impression of the camp was that it was pretty cold and desolate. Daylight didn't improve the view too much but she tried to tell herself that she had only seen the inside of the building at night so far, and that was not a true picture of this part of the world. She wondered if Bonnie had been able to get to sleep in her new surroundings as she wanted her to be bright and ready for the new day, and up to meeting new people and some of the dogs she would be working with. But first there was a really quick and important job to do – to put some posters and an England flag on her bedroom wall to brighten it up! She would have done the same in Bonnie's kennel if she had been allowed to. It was a good job no one cared too much about wallpaper and carpets because the nearest thing to home comforts was air conditioning for the summer and a plug-in heater for the winter.

They arrived in November and it was bitterly cold. Bonnie enjoyed her walk that first morning, getting to know the new terrain and the whole new set of smells that made up her territory. They were to spend the next few weeks getting to know where they were and what was going to be expected of them as a team. They would be using their training in very real situations on the streets and in the homes of Bosnia. They would be searching for weapons, explosives and bomb-making equipment known to be hidden in many houses, factories, farms and buildings throughout the country. It was the Army's job to gather it all in what was known as 'Operation Harvest'.

Bonnie's canine partner was Paddy, a large black Labrador, whose handler was Corporal Alex 'Woody' Wood. The two dogs got on very well, which was good as they were going to be spending at least 12 hours a day in each other's company and much of the time travelling long distances between search areas. Jenny had recently learnt to drive but because Woody was happy to take the wheel Jenny had the opportunity to notice where they were. The beauty of Bosnia could not be appreciated in the bald and false surroundings of the camp. Driving towards the smaller towns and villages with snow on the ground, the scene was idyllic and tranquil. Each community was a mix of trees, thin town houses and low-lying factories and shops, and in the snow it looked like scenes created from white icing on the top of a Christmas cake.

Leaving the camp at 7 a.m. gave Jenny and Woody a chance to exercise the dogs before putting them in the back of the Land Rover and heading out on the road. Paddy was used to what lay ahead each day. He had been in Bosnia nearly six months and was nearing the end of his tour of duty. He knew that as soon as he was in the Land Rover, even before he was in his harness, that he was at work and he settled quickly to his duties.

Bonnie and Jenny were given three weeks to learn the ropes and find their way around. Bonnie was so excited about being in the vehicle that it helped having Paddy there to calm her. Thankfully, as soon as she was out of the vehicle and in harness, she became her true professional self. And Jenny was so proud of her the day she located her first find.

It was during a search of a factory. Bonnie was sent in to the security office while Paddy searched the factory floor. Within minutes Bonnie stopped to indicate that there was something in one of the lockers. Jenny hesitated. It was a tense moment for her. It was all new and she didn't want to report the find to her senior officer if it was a false alarm. She looked at Bonnie. Bonnie looked at her as if to say, 'It's OK … I'm telling the truth. Trust me.' Jenny knew by now that Bonnie was not going to fool her. She knew enough to know that Bonnie had located 'something' and that it should be checked out.

Three times Bonnie indicated the same spot and then Jenny knew for sure that she had to trust her dog. They were told by the factory owner that the key wasn't available but Jenny knew that the locker door had to be opened one way or another. They had to see what was in there. Jenny called for assistance and within no time the locker door was levered open. And there, inside, was an Aladdin's cave stacked with firearms, weapons, ammunition and explosives of all descriptions. The huge cache was brought out of the room piece by piece and stacked ready to be transported away by the bomb disposal team. A hush descended over the entire factory. Someone knew what was in there. Someone knew the danger that everyone had been in while the ammunition was in that locker.

Bonnie had located a huge stock of explosives and ammunition. If any amount of that haul had hit the streets it would have had a very damaging effect on the local community and Bosnia at large. Bonnie received so many cuddles that day for doing such good work, and she rolled on the floor to have her tummy rubbed by all the team. If ever a dog deserved to play with her reward tennis ball it was Bonnie that day. Just in that one find, Bonnie saved many, many lives.

A village could take an entire day to search. Between the two dogs they could search around a hundred houses in a day, maybe more depending on the size of the properties and the number of items found. At first, Jenny and Woody felt as if they were intruding in people's homes but most people made it a painless experience. The locals knew why the British and the US troops were based there, why the dogs were necessary and the reason why the weapons were being confiscated. It was deemed an essential part of securing a much-needed peace. Each household was allowed to retain one firearm, as long as they had a licence to keep it. What they were being asked to hand over was additional weapons, grenades and ammunition. Anything they knew they should not have.

Bonnie saved Jenny's life many, many times over during their four years together and usually she did this thanks to her skills as an explosives search dog. However, the first time she saved Jenny it was in a Land Rover in the snow.

Bonnie and Paddy always travelled as a team with their handlers. The Land Rover became their second home as many of the search locations took days to reach and days to complete. One day they were out on the road, snow covering the entire area, and Bonnie sliced a pad on a front paw during a road search. Jenny had no idea she had been hurt until Bonnie started to limp and then all they could do was return to base for treatment. Bandaged up, Bonnie was grounded for a few days while she recovered. Jenny couldn't help thinking she could have done more to protect her dog but the glass was hidden in the snow. No one could have seen it and it was not common practice for the dogs to wear protective boots in this terrain. But the incident then left Woody and Paddy alone on the road with the search to complete.

They set off early the next morning knowing that Paddy would have to cover Bonnie's portion of the search too. It was very cold and the snow had drifted overnight, leaving a thick white blanket over everything in sight. The warmth of the heater in the Land Rover was the only consolation that morning as Woody made the first tracks of the day in the snow. Suddenly, the Land Rover hit a bump. Woody couldn't control the vehicle as it lurched off the road, falling 300 feet into a ravine.

Silence fell. Nothing, no dog, no man moved in the Land Rover. Fortunately the team was not travelling alone and the others following in another vehicle were able to raise the alarm. Rushing to where the Land Rover had come to rest they discovered Woody had been very badly injured. Paddy was shaken and glad to see the rescuers but he was unhurt. The Land Rover did not survive intact, and there was a shock for Jenny. She was told that the impact of the fall had shunted the car engine into the passenger seat. That was the seat Jenny would have been sitting in if Bonnie had not cut her paw and had had to stay behind. Bonnie and Jenny would have been in that fall too. Jenny didn't want to dwell on that thought and, besides, she was concerned for Woody. His injuries were so severe he had to be airlifted back to the UK. Thankfully he made a full recovery. And Bonnie had saved Jenny's life without knowing it.

The snowfall in Bosnia can be incredibly dramatic. Very often it can be as high as the houses, meaning that homes have to be built on two levels: the lower floor is occupied in the summer and the upper floor in the winter. It's a very sensible plan when you see how the snow can bring life to a standstill. Most of the houses are very homely, although very cramped, and it wasn't unusual for children to sleep wherever they could, anywhere in the house. The houses were very grey on the outside and there was a distinct lack of colour on the inside too. Everything seemed to be hand-crafted, including the blankets and cushions thrown over beds and chairs. Anyone would think it would be impossible to hide anything in such little space but day after day the people proved that it's possible to hide anything anywhere.

Woody's accident meant that Bonnie and Jenny had to carry on the searches alone, sometimes driving many miles to complete the work. Jenny was always surprised by the reaction of the local people to what they were doing. Normally they were very friendly and realized that the military were just doing their job, protecting the civilians. Often the teams were offered coffee to help them warm up after a search and before they had to hit the cold air again, and sometimes they were offered the local homemade liquor. Jenny could never drink it as it was so strong, and the coffee was the same – thick and too strong. But she soon realized that to refuse such kind offers, which sometimes extended to a meal too, would have been very rude. Jenny was always struck by the kindness of people who had to live in such a volatile situation.

There was another side to the weapons confiscation argument, especially from those who felt safer having a weapon to defend themselves, their family and their property. They believed that impounding their weapons left them vulnerable and an easy target. Unsurprisingly, this led to people being very inventive as to where they hid their weapons. On one routine search Bonnie was welcomed into a family's home and fussed by the children. It was an ordinary home, like so very many that Jenny and Bonnie had already searched. Almost immediately however, Bonnie stood by the baby's cot. The baby was asleep.

Jenny didn't want to disturb the baby but Bonnie was insistent. She would not move from the spot. Jenny had no choice; she had to ask the family to turn down the covers or lift the baby away so Bonnie could search. The family became reluctant to cooperate, so Jenny was forced to insist as Bonnie was not going to move. She had found something. After the baby was taken out of the cot, the search team discovered why the family's attitude had changed when Bonnie had sat there. Strapped to the bottom of the cot was a rifle. The family was desperate to keep it as they had already been victims of the conflict: their son had been playing at the front of the house when two rival factions opened fire on each other. Their son was caught in the middle and shot. Once again Bonnie had found what they were there to look for, but on this occasion Jenny couldn't help feeling for the family. They had been touched by the reality of the war and would live with that loss forever.

Moving from location to location to carry out the searches meant Bonnie and Jenny were on the road most of the time. They were often attached to the Royal Engineers or sometimes the Gurkhas to carry out the searches, and having them along was good for morale.

A team could consist of six to eight people and each team would take a village to search throughout the day. Sometimes the villagers would see them arrive and bring their weapons out and hand them over. Jenny remembered a day when she was standing outside a house waiting to start a search, Bonnie at her feet. She was standing as close as she could to Jenny's legs as it was a very cold day. Jenny saw an elderly man wearing a large hat and long coat coming towards her. He was well muffled up against the cold and carrying a shopping bag.

Bonnie was immediately alert. It was her instinct to be suspicious of bags and she wasn't going to let this one pass by. After instructing the man to put the bag down, Jenny stepped away to allow the bomb squad to inspect it. It contained a grenade. The man said he had many more at home for the Army to take away. Every day Jenny was shocked by the familiarity people had with arms and explosives. It was as if they were so used to seeing guns and ammunition lying around that they were not seen as a real danger, not even in the home.

Taking a dog into the houses in Bosnia seemed very natural to Jenny but for some of the local people it was a source of irritation. Dogs in Bosnia stay outdoors and so sometimes the soldiers were offending the people, at the same time as making their homes and communities safer. There were times when Jenny didn't feel safe and was scared for Bonnie too, but she didn't let that prey on her mind. 'If I woke up thinking I could get blown up today, it would be stupid. Much better to concentrate on everything Bonnie was communicating to me and supporting her skills.' Bonnie was Jenny's lifeline and they relied on each other for that.

Bonnie was always very popular with the other soldiers because she was such a lively dog and always went about her work like an eager toddler, bustling about and never stopping until she had found something. One morning in the deep snow a group of Royal Engineers said to Jenny, 'How much do you trust your dog?' 'I'd trust her with my life,' Jenny replied. 'Well then,' they said, 'you can trust her to find your keys!' Covering the keys in oil they threw them into a pile of snow and ice. Bonnie jumped into the heaped-up snow like a crazy gazelle. She was all legs for a few minutes and then, having located the keys, she sat on them.

Everyone was very pleased with her – not least Jenny. It was as if Bonnie was going to show Jenny she was top dog and make up for the early days when she had made Jenny's life so hard!

There was always a lot of competition between the search dog teams. Everyone wanted to be the one to locate the biggest or most impressive haul. Jenny remembered being under the command of a Dutch officer who would say ahead of each search, 'Today is like no other day … today you will find me … a tank!' 'When he saw our raised eyebrows he would say, "OK you will find a lot of weapons." This was because he had worked with the Gurkhas and on one occasion they found a tank, hidden in a cave. They were really hoping to find a helicopter. That was the aim for all of us. The ultimate find. A helicopter.'

What was discovered most of the time was a wide variety of weapons, explosives, bomb-making equipment, shells, ammunition and everything associated with creating maximum damage. The teams never knew what was going to be behind each door, and sometimes, when she was searching alone with Bonnie, Jenny felt vulnerable. In one place they had searched the garage as usual, and they had then moved into the house. Bonnie led the way into a room and there facing them was a man with a gun. For a second Jenny thought that was it. She was dead. The room fell silent. Suddenly, out of nowhere, two soldiers from the Royal Engineers appeared and challenged the man. He said he meant no harm and immediately gave up his weapon. The incident was over in a second, but for Jenny it was a moment in time that she could never forget. She held Bonnie tightly and told her, 'Bonnie, we're all doing a dangerous job and life could be there one second and gone the next. We've got to look after each other.'

The searches were routine but every now and then something happened to make the handlers aware of their own mortality. Jenny's duty was to Queen and country and her loyalty was to her fellow soldiers and dogs. 'Bonnie looked after me as I looked after her.' This really is teamwork. A bond created and never to be forgotten.

In some ways Bosnia was a trial run for what was to come.

* * *

After almost six months in Bosnia, Jenny found herself heading to Germany with Bonnie for a wind-down period. It was also a quarantine slot for Bonnie. The thought of a posting to Iraq would have probably scared Jenny before Bosnia but it had been a good introduction to the kind of work she would be doing with Bonnie every day and it was the kind of challenge Jenny felt she needed.

By June 2004 they were ready to head out and Jenny had her orders to collect her desert kit before starting their preparation for 'the Sandy Place'. While Bonnie continued to go through her paces in Germany and sharpen her skills, Jenny was sent to the classroom for five days. She had to learn what to do if she was challenged in a vehicle on the roads in Iraq, and gain an understanding of the different languages spoken within the country and the culture and customs. In just two weeks they were to be ready for Iraq.

Full body armour plus helmet were to be worn on the flight. The plane was a late-night flight into Basra and it was heading for a hostile zone. The lights were dimmed in the cabin as the Hercules started its descent.

As it did Jenny suddenly became aware of the potential dangers she and Bonnie would be facing. Jenny knew she would feel happier once Bonnie was in her arms again, and clearly Bonnie felt the same because she got the warmest welcome possible from the big soppy black Labrador! What Jenny wasn't expecting was the wall of heat that hit her as they stepped off the plane.

Jenny could tell the heat was going to be a problem for her, and Bonnie was suffering too. But that wasn't the only problem. Part of the welcoming party that day was also a dreaded camel spider. This spider injects its victim with venom that numbs the limbs while it sets about eating the flesh. Jenny had heard of these from her big brother but it didn't stop her being totally terrified when one appeared in her shadow at the airport. Jenny saw the spider and ran before she realized what it was; fortunately, it didn't catch either her or Bonnie.

They arrived in June and, as soon as they landed, Jenny understood why everyone was handing her bottles of cold water for her and Bonnie – plus the factor 50 sunscreen. The first battle they were both going to fight was against the heat. For the first week it was all about getting to know where they were and taking the necessary steps to gain Bonnie's licence to work on the ground. They had five sections of this programme to complete and, as always, Bonnie lapped up the opportunity to show off her skills. It's not easy being a black Labrador in the sort of heat that takes your breath away but Bonnie was coping as well as could be expected. Night was the worst time, so if Jenny could find a place to lie on the floor in a breeze then they would do that just to get comfortable, and do the same in the daytime under the trees.

Basra Airport became Bonnie's playground and the base for the first search activities. It was also the base for the Royal Engineers who, as in Bosnia, would be working with Jenny and Bonnie on the ground. A Land Rover with air-conditioning became Bonnie's favourite way to travel. Even taking the early shift, leaving the base at 7 a.m., the air-con was a real luxury; if they went out later it was a necessity. If they were unlucky they would have to travel in a Warrior armoured vehicle. The Warrior was an essential part of the equipment for travelling in the cities, or in any built-up area, but

Bonnie didn't like its claustrophobic environment. She knew she was safe because she was with Jenny but she was always irritable and nervous for the entire journey. There was no air-con and Bonnie had her black coat to cope with; the humans were no better off, with their full desert camouflage, body armour and webbing to contend with as well as the supply of water for Bonnie to drink and to tip over her body. The heat in Iraq was oppressive and everyone suffered the effects. A trip in a Warrior was only brightened for Bonnie when there was a find at the end of it. Very often a day would end with a collection of finds to be gathered by the explosives disposal unit and destroyed. On days like that, Bonnie was a happy dog.

It did not take long for Bonnie and the rest of the search dogs to become the centre of attention for enemy activities. The dogs were fast becoming too effective at their job and therefore a threat to terrorist activities. 'It was something our superiors were aware of and we had to take every precaution to safeguard the dogs while we were out on searches.' They may have been listed as Army supplies and 'equipment', but the dogs were providing valuable support to the front-line troops and kept people alive with each successful detection of an explosive device. Jenny knew that Bonnie was relying on her to keep her safe in every situation, so they were often together 24 hours a day to work and to protect each other. Once it was known the dogs were a potential target for the sniper's bullet, they became more treasured than ever before.

The ever-oppressive heat was a constant battle for Bonnie and for Jenny too. It came to the point where the only real respite was travelling by helicopter. Travelling between the city and the desert, the helicopter came into its own. Fortunately Bonnie loved helicopters, but they did not get to travel in them too often because most of their work took place in the city, and it was the city that held the most fear for Jenny.

One night Jenny remembered clearly was when they were sent to search a roadside just outside Basra. They knew it had to be a quick but thorough search before they were noticed. Suddenly they came under fire. As bullets zipped past them they knew that they couldn't run or hide away from the ambush as Bonnie still had both sides of the road to search. If there was a roadside bomb the devastation of losing colleagues would have been too hard to bear. They had to stay on. A cover man joined them. Where he came from Jenny didn't see but he was a godsend as he fired on the attackers. 'Pull back! Pull back!' came the order. Bonnie did as she was told but a moment later she was back on the search. The firing intensified as she continued and Jenny could smell the heat and the metal of the bullets. Bonnie searched on despite the intimidation of the bullets, but as they approached a wall Jenny gestured to Bonnie to join her. She figured that if they could hold out there for a few minutes the gunfire would cease, which would give them both a chance to have some calm. It was the terror of being able to hear the bullets but not see them. They just knew they were out there, coming at you out of the dark. 'Faint darts of light spat into the darkness and I watched them disappear in the distance. There was no relief like it. To hear the bullet crack and then realize it wasn't for you – this time.'

They would have worked on but they followed the order to 'pull back', knowing the road had been searched. Bonnie had done her job, and had made that area a little safer and clear for the armoured vehicles to pass through. Roadside bombs were the hidden killers and if a vehicle was caught in an explosion it could kill and maim up to five people. Bonnie and her canine colleagues were saving lives every day they were on duty. It was not difficult work, and it was always something she had been trained for. She had also been 'gun tested' – she didn't run at the sound of any firearm. She just quietly and quickly sniffed her way through the job in hand and did it well. If she had not been a confident dog Jenny would not be around to tell the tale.

The rivers Euphrates and Tigris flow into Shatt al-Arab waterway, which provided another means for the terrorists to transport goods and ammunition. Bonnie loved searching the boats because she loved being near the water. On a river search one night Bonnie was ahead of Jenny, darting back to her at intervals to report in, as she should. But if Bonnie found water to wade in then she would do that rather than run back. On this particular night Bonnie thought her luck was in when she saw a pool. A big, shiny pool waiting for a hot and bothered dog to jump in – so she did! Unfortunately this 'pool' was a pool of oil. Clambering out of the black sludge, Bonnie looked at Jenny as if to say, 'I'm sorry, I have no idea why I did that!' But it was not unusual for Bonnie to jump into mud thinking it was water too. Mud, oil and water – not the best combination to have to clean off a dog after a long, hard day working under fire.

The US Army stationed at Camp Dogwood also had a canine search unit, but at the time they had only five dogs. This meant that the British dogs were sometimes sent to help out. Jenny enjoyed working with the Americans for a while as they had a different way of organizing searches, and their ration packs were more exciting than the British versions. The camp was on the front line of the action near Fallujah. The Black Watch infantry regiment and a 20-strong unit of the Royal Engineers were stationed there, and it was a magnet for stray dogs. Set in the desert, Camp Dogwood was made up of five buildings built on a square with 'stag positions' or look-out posts on top of each building. Each was manned by two people; a formidable-looking building, as it was meant to be.

Patrolling the area was not easy and best executed by air. Being on the front line it was no surprise that on Bonnie and Jenny's first night the camp came under attack from rocket propelled grenades (RPGs). Jenny had never heard the noise before but it is one she is never likely to forget. The ominous whistling was unnerving for Bonnie too.

Bonnie was happy enough finding a cache of arms and she knew that there would always be a treat – maybe a tennis ball game but maybe, as happened in Camp Dogwood, sweets, chocolate bars and noodle snacks. Every evening Bonnie would search the perimeter of the camp and each time there would be someone to give her a treat. She always did a very good act of looking hungry and adorable and it always worked. Jenny enjoyed sharing her ration pack with Bonnie, cooking her meal and then splitting it between the two of them. It was a good job they weren't stationed there for very long as Jenny feared Bonnie would need to go on a diet. As it was, Bonnie enjoyed life on the camp, with access to her bed, her food, the people who adored her and gave her treats, and the chance to sleep when she wanted. The dogs worked hard but they were treated well. They shared the fear of the explosions and the treats afterwards – Army life on the front line.

British troops had been stationed in Iraq since 2003, and the supporters of Saddam Hussein were still taking lives with bombs and the sniper's bullet. When Jenny and Bonnie were transferred back to Shaibah Logistics Base near the Kuwait border, news came in of two Engineers who had lost their legs in an explosion. Without the dog search teams the injuries and fatalities would have been far more frequent. Jenny knew the value of the work she was performing with Bonnie, but it added to the pressure. Trust in Bonnie was paramount but it was probably best that Bonnie was oblivious to the tension. As they moved from camp to camp Bonnie built a reputation for being a dog that got the job done and who did it quickly and thoroughly, and Jenny was immensely proud of her. It was not the way the relationship started but Jenny had forgiven Bonnie for that a long time ago.

Jenny had one more month left in Iraq and the intensity of the searching was still high. The main road through to Basra was always a target for bomb attacks and so the road and vehicle checks were a constant part of the job. Bonnie would do road searches for half a day, and then rest and go back to another duty if she was not sent back for a second round if someone had been sent elsewhere. The vehicle checks were very controlled. A sign saying: 'Do not pass this sign' reminded drivers to pull over and prepare for the vehicle to be searched. One time Bonnie and Jenny were on check duty when a vehicle passed and then continued up a hill, avoiding the check. Jenny immediately radioed ahead to say the vehicle was heading towards the next checkpoint. Not content with seeing the vehicle pass by, Bonnie ran on after it. She knew that it should have stopped.

Jenny raised her rifle and prepared for a challenge and called Bonnie back to her. Suddenly the vehicle swung round and came back in their direction. Then Jenny could see the man driving had children in the car. How could he put them in such a vulnerable position, she wondered. It was a road check with armed guards. Forced to wait and surrounded by armed soldiers, the man submitted to the road check. He was not carrying anything suspicious. For all the checks Jenny and Bonnie carried out without any bother, there were also those like this one where lives were at risk on both sides.

Being a female handler there were certain places Jenny could not search in Iraq. One of these was monasteries. Usually she would wait in the vehicle with Bonnie for the men to return. There were other searches she would rather not have done, such as the animal yards. The vast areas where farm animals were herded were, in most cases, pools of animal excrement. Going in up to her ankles was bad enough but that meant Bonnie was in deeper. It was one of the places all the handlers hated to search, which was why they had to be searched so thoroughly. Derelict buildings were also places everyone would prefer to avoid if they could, as there was always a fear of what and who could be inside. But this was all part of the job and one Jenny and her colleagues got used to. Every building, car check or roadside check probably looked the same to Bonnie, but they entered each situation trusting each other and they were right to do so. They survived, and thanks to Bonnie's skills, many other people survived too.

When Jenny's tour came to an end she had to leave Bonnie behind, until there was a handler and a suitable flight to get her back to Germany. It was three months before Jenny saw her again but the dog hadn't forgotten her. As soon as she stepped into the kennels Bonnie was all over her, just as she used to be. It didn't seem to matter that she had been working with different handlers while they had been apart. It was as if Jenny had just stepped outside for a moment rather than them parting three months previously.

Bonnie didn't know it but Jenny was only back to work with her until a new handler could be found to take her on. It seemed very odd to Jenny that her dog – because she always felt that Bonnie was her dog – would be with someone else. She really didn't want to think about it and she felt she wasn't ready to talk to her about it, and she definitely was not ready to say goodbye.

Jenny had been assigned a young drug detection dog, called Casper. The two dogs got on so well together Jenny couldn't help thinking: Why can't I keep them both? Why do I have to let Bonnie go? 'We had been together four years and helped each other through some very difficult times. She had been my work partner, my best friend and the "person" closest to me through the cold nights in Bosnia and the heat of Iraq. Always there with a smile on her face and a wagging tail. Always ready to protect me in a crisis. Bonnie was a dog in a million and now I had to say goodbye to my best friend.'

Jenny had no idea how she was going to do this. It was the hardest thing ever for her to do. She decided to take it back to how the relationship started, with a walk together and a chat along the way.

I though if I could pretend everything was normal then Bonnie wouldn't know any different when I put her back in her kennel and walked away. It was the worst time of my life. Bonnie was much too intelligent to be fooled by me. She knew I was leaving and she heaped her huge self on top of me, I'm sure to make me stay. We played our game of rough and tumble and I just about managed to squeeze myself from under the lump of a Labrador and pull myself together ... It was the hardest goodbye of them all.

A year later, Jenny received a call from her old boss. He told her that Bonnie was due to be retired and asked her if she would like to take her on. Jenny's heart leapt with excitement! To be back with Bonnie would be a dream come true. But then she had to think about the practical side of things: she was living with her parents and her father had just acquired a dog. Although her mother said she could have her Jenny knew that it wouldn't be fair as she was about to be posted overseas again. She knew that it would not have been fair on her parents, and it wouldn't be fair on Bonnie either. Reluctantly she had to say that she was sorry, she couldn't take Bonnie.

Two months after that difficult decision was made Jenny received a wonderful letter. It was from the family who had adopted Bonnie and taken her to their hearts. She had been adopted by an Army officer and his family who obviously loved Bonnie so much that they had to share it with Jenny. The letter explained all the mischief she got up to and said how much they loved her for her naughtiness! There were photographs and drawings of the smiley Labrador Jenny remembered so well. Jenny was so happy for Bonnie in her retirement. She was a dog in a million.

Epilogue

Heroism is not a quality confined to human beings. Animals are capable of courage too. Those who doubt even the idea of animal bravery should speak to a Serviceman or woman whose life has been saved by an animal's actions during conflict. They will tell you that animals are indeed capable of incredible bravery and inspirational devotion to those around them. The dogs covered in this book echo that sentiment loud and clear.

Delving into books and researching wartime documents is one way to glean a picture of most theatres of conflict. Talking to the veterans who fought those battles adds the colour and the detail to the scene and out of that very often come the stories of the many mascots that were adopted by soldiers, sailors and airmen for one reason or another. In the case of Judy, the Japanese POW dog, her saviour was a young leading aircraftsman, Frank Williams, who one day shared his meagre rice ration with the starving English pointer and in that one gesture of generosity made a friend for life.

It's partnerships like the one forged between Judy and Frank Williams that highlight the intense level of devotion that possibly only exists within the confines of war. The dogs presented here all have two things in common: war and their own special 'owner'. Canadian mascot dog Gander had the entire 1st Battalion of the Royal Rifles of Canada to watch out for him but it was his handler, Fred Kelly, who showered, fed, groomed and looked after the huge, faithful Newfoundland. Rats, the 'soldier dog' of Northern Ireland, chose to adopt the soldiers of 42 Commando Royal Marines in 1978 and followed them back to base. But it wasn't until he met Grenadier Guardsman Sergeant Tim Fielding that Rats (or Rat, as he was to the Grenadiers) selected one man for his partner. The sadness for Rats was the constant change of regiments that necessitated a constant change of friends.

It's almost certain that these special partnerships radiate their affection to the benefit of the entire company. In this book, the five dogs directly affected and protected their five owners or handlers, but they also protected every individual they served alongside. For explosives search dogs like Bonnie (and springer spaniel Buster, featured on the cover with his handler Sergeant Danny Morgan), one successful 'find' saves not only the lives of the soldiers on duty but the entire population in the vicinity of the search. The skill and bravery of these dogs touches hundreds of lives.

The telling of these five stories is just a taster; there are thousands of other dogs who have been hailed as heroes over years of warfare, and there are so many stories of canine heroism, and some cases where dogs have been decorated for their bravery in conflict. The PDSA Dickin Medal, recognized as the animals'

Victoria Cross, honours conspicuous bravery in battle. To date 26 dogs have received the award since its institution in 1943. Its most recent recipient, in February 2007, was an explosives search dog called Sadie, awarded for bravery in Afghanistan. The medal is unique, as are all its recipients.

Heroism appears in many guises, and that includes the four-legged heroes in fur coats. *The Dog that Saved My Life* is a small tribute to a large contingent of soldier, sailor and airdogs who give their all even when there seems little more to give. They give because they want to and to partners who would risk the same for them in the front line.

In wartime a dog can be an iconic reminder of the comforts of home, the fireside warmth of family so far away. Dogs, the eternal levellers, the non-judgemental companions capable of bravery beyond the call of duty, can display a quality of character that distinguishes the extraordinary from the ordinary, provides comfort where there is pain and calm where there is confusion. A dog can do all of this by just being – a dog.

The inspiring hero dogs that captured the hearts of all the men and women that they worked alongside:

Gander, who travelled with his soldier friends from Canada to save their lives in Hong Kong. IMAGE © EILEEN ELMS.

Judy, the only dog to be officially registered as a prisoner of war. IMAGE © PDSA.

Rats, a small dog with a big personality, recorded as the longest-serving member of the British Army in South Armagh. IMAGE © TOPFOTO/PA.

Caesar, the Australian Tracker dog and Peter, his handler (right).
IMAGE © PETER HARAN.

Bonnie and handler Jenny Chester, serving on the front
line in Fallujah. IMAGE © PA.